Shengfa Gao

Message Number Check and Message Rearranging Theory and Protocols

AF141104

Shengfa Gao

Message Number Check and Message Rearranging Theory and Protocols

In Rollback Recovery of Distributed Systems

LAP LAMBERT Academic Publishing

Impressum / Imprint

Bibliografische Information der Deutschen Nationalbibliothek: Die Deutsche Nationalbibliothek verzeichnet diese Publikation in der Deutschen Nationalbibliografie; detaillierte bibliografische Daten sind im Internet über http://dnb.d-nb.de abrufbar.

Alle in diesem Buch genannten Marken und Produktnamen unterliegen warenzeichen-, marken- oder patentrechtlichem Schutz bzw. sind Warenzeichen oder eingetragene Warenzeichen der jeweiligen Inhaber. Die Wiedergabe von Marken, Produktnamen, Gebrauchsnamen, Handelsnamen, Warenbezeichnungen u.s.w. in diesem Werk berechtigt auch ohne besondere Kennzeichnung nicht zu der Annahme, dass solche Namen im Sinne der Warenzeichen- und Markenschutzgesetzgebung als frei zu betrachten wären und daher von jedermann benutzt werden dürften.

Bibliographic information published by the Deutsche Nationalbibliothek: The Deutsche Nationalbibliothek lists this publication in the Deutsche Nationalbibliografie; detailed bibliographic data are available in the Internet at http://dnb.d-nb.de.

Any brand names and product names mentioned in this book are subject to trademark, brand or patent protection and are trademarks or registered trademarks of their respective holders. The use of brand names, product names, common names, trade names, product descriptions etc. even without a particular marking in this works is in no way to be construed to mean that such names may be regarded as unrestricted in respect of trademark and brand protection legislation and could thus be used by anyone.

Coverbild / Cover image: www.ingimage.com

Verlag / Publisher:
LAP LAMBERT Academic Publishing
ist ein Imprint der / is a trademark of
OmniScriptum GmbH & Co. KG
Heinrich-Böcking-Str. 6-8, 66121 Saarbrücken, Deutschland / Germany
Email: info@lap-publishing.com

Herstellung: siehe letzte Seite /
Printed at: see last page
ISBN: 978-3-8473-4839-9

Zugl. / Approved by: Jinan,Shandong University,2014

If you are not confined to something existing, you will find a very bright future.

This monograph is dedicated to the educators and researchers who are working on the first line of teaching and researching.

Shengfa Gao

Acknowledgment

I would like to express my appreciation to my students, Jing Cai, Fengyan Zuo, Yanan Wang, Cuiying Liu and Chuanqing Shi, for cooperating with me to finish the project of Natural Science Foundation of Shandong Province of China No. Z2008G03.

I am indebted to thank Wang Hua and Ju Lei for useful discussions regarding the theory and algorithm in this monograph.

I am also indebted to thank to Jia Zhiping, Li Xin, Dai Hongjun, Zhang Ruihua, Li Feng, LI Yibin and Yang xiaoyan, for their helping in my research.

I would like to express my appreciation to Mr. Ghenadie Braghis for helping me to finish this monograph.

I am grateful to my daughter Yaxian Gao and my niece Guannan Gao for their useful help in my work.

Shengfa Gao

Feb, 2014

Preface

Many techniques have been used to add reliability to the distributed systems; rollback-recovery is the most economic way to acquire such property of the distributed systems.

Rollback-recovery treats the distributed system composed as a number of processes that communicate through a network. Generally speaking, the system achieves fault tolerance by using a stable storage device to save each process's recovery information during its failure-free execution. Upon process's failure, the system restarts the computation from a state that decided by each process's saved information. As it needs not restart from its initial state, thereby the system reduces the amount of lost computation upon system failure. The information being used to recover failures depends on recovery protocol to be used. It may include, at least the stable states of the participating processes which called checkpoints, logs of the interactions with input and output devices, events that occur to each process, and messages exchanged among the processes.

By if the determinant [1] of a message is logged to stable storage; the approaches of rollback recovery can be classified into two categories [2]: checkpoint based rollback-recovery and message log based rollback-recovery. Different rollback-recovery offers different tradeoffs about performance in process failure free execution, simplicity of recovery, latency of output committing, and the extent of rollback, etc.

In previous studies of rollback recovery, the protocols are nearly all based on the analysis of the casual dependent relations among message receipt and sending events, or process state intervals. As the tracking casual relation among events is very complex, it is very difficult to find a way to simultaneously obtain good performance of process execution, simplicity of recovery, etc. Chapter one will give detail.

It is the main purpose of this monograph to discover some unknown properties of the distributed systems and improve the rollback recovery algorithms and protocols.

In chapter two, we propose the message number check theory and methods to determine the consistency of a global state to replace the analysis of casual relation among events or state intervals. Thus the issue of the consistency of the global state is changed from by the relation analysis to by the mathematical methods.

It is default that the message receipt order cannot be recovered if it is lost in previous message logging protocols. In chapter three, to address the problem of the message receipt order loss, we propose the message rearranging theory and methods to recover the loss of message receipt order upon process failure.

In chapter four, two examples of a message logging protocol based on message rearranging and an algorithm to calculate recovery line are given to explain how to use the theory and methods in chapter two and chapter three.

Shengfa Gao
Jinan, China
Feb, 2014

Contents

Acknowledgment...

Preface...

Illustrations ....

Tables..

Chapter 1 Rollback Recovery..1

    Summary 1

    1.1 Some Concepts in Rollback Recovery 1

        1.1.1 System Model 1

        1.1.2 Consistent Global State 2

        1.1.3 PWD Assumption 2

        1.1.4 Message Replaying 3

        1.1.5 Output Committing 6

    1.2 Checkpoint based Rollback Recovery 7

        1.2.1 Coordinated Checkpointing 7

        1.2.2 Uncoordinated Checkpointing..7

        1.2.3 Communication-Induced Checkpointing 9

    1.3 Log based Rollback Recovery..10

        1.3.1 *Always-no-orphan* Consistency Condition...10

        1.3.2 Pessimistic Logging 11

        1.3.3 Optimistic Logging 13

        1.3.4 Causal Logging 14

Chapter 2 Message Number Check Theory...16

    Summary 16

    2.1 Global State Function of Time Variable 16

    2.2 Global State Function of Clock Variable 17

    2.3 Message Number Check Theory...18

Chapter 3 Message Rearranging Theory...23

    Summary 23

    3.1 Introduction 23

    3.2 Always-happens-before Relation 24

    3.3 Equivalent Message Sequence..25

    3.4 Method to Rearrange Message 26

Chapter 4 Corresponding Protocol..31

    Summary 31

    4.1 A Protocol based on Message Rearrange..31

        4.1.1 Introduction..31

        4.1.2 System Model 31

        4.1.3 Main Data Structure 31

        4.1.4 Description of the Protocol 32

        4.1.5 Correctness of the Protocol 34

        4.1.6 Performance of the Protocol 35

    4.2 Find Recovery Line by Message Number Check..36

        4.2.1 Introduction..36

4.2.2 System Modal and Main Data Structure 37

4.2.3 Description of the Algorithm 37

4.2.4 Correctness of the Algorithm 38

4.2.5 Comparison with other Algorithms 39

References 40

Illustrations

1.1 In-transit message

1.2 Inconsistent and consistent global state

1.3 State intervals after receiving messages

1.4 Message replaying system

1.5 (a) q fails before sending m_2 (b) q fails after sending m_2

1.6 q and r fail before logging m_5 and m_6

1.7 State interval in which sending an output message

1.8 Rollback of the processes in the system

1.9 A z-cycle: m_3, $C_{1,2}$, m_4

1.10 An orphan process p_3

1.11 Only one process depends on the message receipt event

1.12 Only failed processes rollback

1.13 Orphan processes p and q rollback

1.14 q and r recovered under guidance of p

1.15 Antecedence graph of p at time t

2.1 Volatile consistent global states at time t_1, t_2 and t_3

2.2 Consistency of global state determined by message number

2.3 T matrix of the distributed system

2.4 Improved vector logical clocks of a system

2.5 A T matrix of a system

2.6 U matrix of the distributed system

2.7 Sending vectors of a system

2.8 A U matrix of a system

2.9 An orphan message in $G(t_1, t_2)$

2.10 Vector logic clock and sending vector of a system

2.11 A system with Non-FIFO channel

3.1 A distributed system consists of p, q and r

3.2 *Always-happens-before* relation among events

3.3 Possibly receipt message sequence

3.4 Improved logic clocks of p, q, r

3.5 $S(m_j)$ indirectly precedes $R(m_i)$

3.6 Receipt order determined by sender's logic clock

3.7 *LC* is recovered from the information in stable storage

4.1 An example of our protocol

4.2 Message log of the system

4.3 p and r go on running

4.4 An example of the algorithm

Tables

4.1 Comparison among message logging protocols

Chapter 1 Rollback Recovery

Summary

Rollback recovery plays a significant role in reliability of distributed system design. This chapter first introduces some concept widely used in rollback recovery, and makes clear the mechanism of some important technique, such as the message replaying, output committing. Then it introduces various rollback recovery protocols published in the literature, and sums up the advantages and disadvantages of them by analyzing their implement theory, technique feature and protocol instance.

1.1 Some Concepts in Rollback Recovery

1.1.1 System Model

A distributed system consists of many processes which run on many nodes and communicate only through messages. Each process executes on a node in the system. The node fails according to the fail stop model [3] which the crashed process on it halts its computation with losing all contents of its volatile memory.

There is a distributed stable storage that every process can always access, which persists beyond processor failures, thereby supporting recovery from failures of an arbitrary number of processors.

Processes have no global memory and global clock. The system is asynchronous; each process executes at its own speed and communicates with each other only through messages at finite but arbitrary transmission delays.

The communication subsystem may be reliable or unreliable. If it is assumed to be reliable, it delivers message in First-Input-First-Output (FIFO) order. In this case, if the receiver process fails, the in-transit message must be re-sent after it is recovered by the system to preserve the semantics of reliable communication subsystem [2]. For instance, in Figure 1.1, at time t ($t_1 \leq t < t_2$), message m is an in-transit message, because it is on the way to process p at that time period. Suppose process p fails at "x", after it is recovered from failure the system must re-send this message m to p if under reliable communication subsystem assumption.

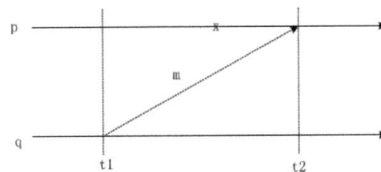

Figure1.1 In-transit message

If the communication subsystem is assumed to be unreliable, then it can lose, duplicate, or reorder the messages. In this case, the in-transit message will be lost if the receiver process fails before it receives this message. Under unreliable communication subsystem assumption, the recovery protocol needs to detect these lost, duplicated and reordered

1

messages and correct the errors among them.

1.1.2 Consistent Global State

A global state of a distributed system is a collection of the state of each process in the system and the state of communication channel.

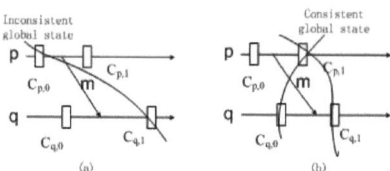

Figure1.2 Inconsistent and consistent global state

A consistent global state is one in which, if the state of a process contains a message receipt event, then the state of corresponding sender process also contains the sending event of that message [4].

Suppose the system consists of two processes p and q, Figure 1.2 shows the examples of consistent global state and inconsistent global state. A local checkpoint is a process state which saved in stable storage at some time during process failure free execution. In Figure 1.2 (a) the global state which consists of process checkpoint $C_{p,0}$ and $C_{q,1}$ is inconsistent, because $C_{q,1}$ records the m's receipt event, $C_{p,0}$ does not record the m's sending event. Such a state is impossible in any failure free and correct process execution. But, the global states shown in Figure 1.2 (b) are all consistent. Look at the global state reflected by checkpoint $C_{p,1}$ and $C_{q,0}$, this state is consistent. Because it shows a situation in which the message m has been sent by the sender and is still traveling across the network, in fact m is an in-transit message. The global state which consists of $C_{p,1}$ and $C_{q,1}$ is also consistent, because the sending event of m is recorded by $C_{p,1}$, the receipt event of m is also recorded by $C_{q,1}$, in fact it is a strongly consistent global state [6].

1.1.3 PWD Assumption

Log-based rollback-recovery relies on the piecewise deterministic (PWD) assumption [5]. PWD postulates that all nondeterministic events a process executes can be identified and the information necessary to replay each nondeterministic event can be logged.

By logging the nondeterministic events and replaying them in their exact original order during recovery, a process can deterministically recreate its state before failure, even if this state has not been saved to stable storage.

Nondeterministic events in a log based rollback recovery protocol may be changed on different assumption. They may include receiving messages, receiving input from the outside world, or undergoing an internal state transfer within a process based on some nondeterministic action such as the receipt of an interrupt [2]. But, the message sending event is not a nondeterministic event, for it deterministically takes place in a state interval which is started by a nondeterministic event.

Under PWD assumption, the execution of each process is divided into discrete state intervals by the message receipt events. Each state interval contains a deterministic event sequence which ended with the next nondeterministic event. The execution of a process within a state interval is completely determined by the nondeterministic event and by the contents of this event.

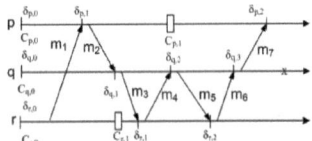

Figure 1.3 State intervals after receiving messages

As shown in Figure 1.3, suppose a distributed system consists of process p, q and r. Where, $C_{x,y}$ denotes yth checkpoint of process x. $\delta_{x,z}$ denotes zth state interval of process x. If PWD assumption holds, process p enters its initial state interval $\delta_{p,0}$ after it is started. After receiving message m_1 from r, p enters its next state interval $\delta_{p,1}$. Accordingly, each process enters its next state interval after receiving a message as Figure 1.3 shown.

1.1.4 Message Replaying

Under PWD assumption, if all the information of the nondeterministic events is logged to stable storage before process failure, recovery protocol can recover a failed process by replaying these events. Replaying means re-executing the process by driving it to execute the nondeterministic events saved in stable storage.

Suppose the nondeterministic event is only the message receipt event. Let *m.source* denote the sender process identification of message m, *m.ssn* denote sending sequence number assigned by the sender to m. Let *m.dest* denote receiver process identification, *m.rsn* denote message receiving sequence number assigned by receiver process. The tuple <*m.source, m.ssn, m.dest, m.rsn*> unequivocally determines m and the order in which m was delivered by the process. We refer to this tuple as the determinant of message m.

Under log based recovery protocols, the determinant of each message is saved in stable storage in a process failure free execution. Thus, a process can be recovered by replaying the message receipt events saved in stable storage upon process failure.

During the message replaying, failed process accepts the messages sent by the recovery system with their original receipt order; meanwhile it may send some messages to other processes. The messages sent by a process during message replaying are duplicate messages, for they have been received and processed by other processes in their normal execution. Thus, such messages must be detected and ignored by their receivers, or must not be allowed by the system to be transmitted again during recovery.

From the message replaying mentioned above, we could have found that the execution of a failed process is driven by message receipt events, which is not controlled by the distributed system itself. To depict the message replaying more accurately, we model the message replaying system as follow:

3

- A recovery manager.
- A finite number of processes denoted as p_k, k=1, 2,... n.

As shown in Figure 1.4, recovery manager is used to restart a failed process p_k from its checkpoint. During the message replaying, recovery manager retrieves the messages by their determinants saved in message log and re-sends them to a failed process p_k.

Processes p_k, k=1, 2,... n, are connected by communication channel. Each process p_k, or may receive messages from the recovery manager and send messages to another process during recovery, or may receive or send messages (such as m_j) from or to another process in its normal execution.

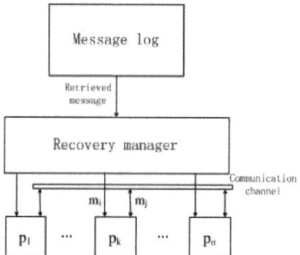

Figure 1.4 Message replaying system

During the message replaying before reaching the maximum recoverable state [7] of the system, a failed process will re-send some messages that it has sent during its normal execution. These messages are duplicated messages, thus must be detected and ignored by their receivers, or must not be allowed by the system to be transmitted again during recovery.

An example of message replaying refers to Figure 1.3. Suppose q fails at "x" after all the message receipt events in the system are logged to message log, just as pessimistic message log protocols do. During recovery, q is rolled back to checkpoint $C_{q,0}$, then it replays the receipt events of m_2, m_4 and m_6. That is, q is restarted from its checkpoint $C_{q,0}$; then the messages of m_2, m_4 and m_6 are retrieved from message log and are re-sent to q by recovery manager. Suppose the delivery history of m_3, m_5 and m_7 has been recorded by p and r in their normal execution, they discard these messages after they receive these messages.

Another example, as shown in Figure 1.5 (a), suppose process q fails at "x" after message m_1 is logged to stable storage and the execution of state interval is not atomic. As m_2 has not been sent by q, this message must have not been received by p. After it receives m_2, p should not discard m_2. On the contrary, in Figure 1.5 (b), m_2 must be discarded by p during message replaying; because the state interval started by m_1 receipt event has been fully executed.

A state interval is recoverable [7] if there is sufficient information to replay the execution up to that state interval despite any future failures in the system.

The maximum recoverable state (MRS) [7] is defined as the state to which the system will be recovered if a failure occurs. Examples of maximum recoverable state are shown in Figure 1.5, in (a) the maximum recoverable state is before $\delta_{q,1}$ because $\delta_{q,1}$ in (a) is not recoverable, in (b) the maximum recoverable state is after $\delta_{q,1}$ because $\delta_{q,1}$ in (b) is

4

recoverable.

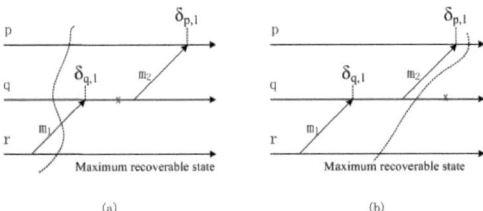

(a)   (b)

Figure1.5 (a) q fails before sending m_2 (b) q fails after sending m_2

From the instance above, it can be found that the execution of failed process will be divided into two stages by the maximum recoverable state:

1. Before reaching the MRS, the messages saved in the message log are replayed by the recovery manager and the failed processes. In this stage, the messages sent by a failed process should be discarded by the receiver process.

2. After reaching the MRS, the failed processes will begin their normal execution; any message sent by them should not be discarded by the receiver processes.

Different from the example shown in Figure 1.3, some recovery protocols may allow the processes in the system to delay the action of logging a message after receiving it. So once some processes fail, some messages may have not been logged to stable storage; this may occur in optimistic message logging protocols.

For example, in Figure 1.6, suppose processes q and r fail at "x" before m_5 and m_6 are logged to stable storage. In this case, the maximum recoverable state is just after the state interval $\delta_{q,2}$ and $\delta_{r,1}$ and before $\delta_{p,2}$, $\delta_{q,3}$ and $\delta_{r,2}$; $\delta_{p,2}$, $\delta_{q,3}$ and $\delta_{r,2}$ are executed in processes normal execution.

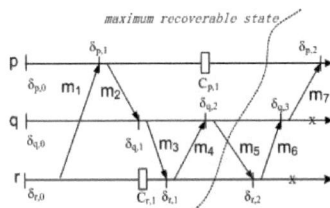

Figure 1.6 q and r fail before logging m_5 and m_6

If there is more than one process fail, then a failed process and the recovery manager may send the same message to another failed process. In this case, because the failed process needs only receive messages sent by the recovery manager during recovery, it is not reasonable for the failed process to receive messages from another failed process. Thus, the message sent by a failed process to another failed process must not be allowed by the system to be transmitted again during recovery. For instance, in Figure 1.6, process r and the recovery manager may send the same message m_4

5

to process q during the message replaying. The message m_4 sent by r must not be allowed to be transmitted during recovery.

1.1.5 Output Committing

A process in a distributed system may often interact with input and output peripherals, such as by keyboard to input data, by printer to show the result of the computation. Some output peripherals can be modeled as a special process which is called "outside world process" (OWP) [2], such as the printer.

The OWP has such property that the same output message must be outputted once and only once, so the recovery protocol must make sure the state output massage been sent will be recovered regardless of any future failure.

To hold the property of OWP, in log based rollback recovery the state interval in which the output message is sent must be recoverable. That is, there must be enough information to replay the execution up to this state interval in spite of any future failure.

For instance, in Figure 1.7, suppose all messages m_1, m_2 and m_3 are logged before the p's failure and the execution of state interval is not atomic. In Figure 1.7 (a), $\delta_{p,1}$ is recoverable, because it is completely executed. But in Figure 1.7 (b), $\delta_{p,1}$ is not recoverable, because it cannot be recovered, the maximum recoverable state is just before $\delta_{p,1}$.

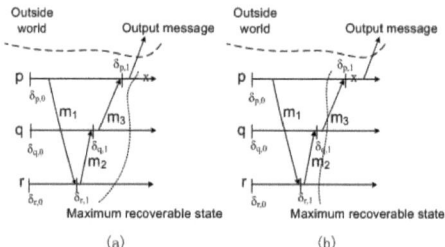

Figure 1.7 State interval in which sending an output message

Definition 1-1. When an output message is sent to OWP, it is committing-able if the property of OWP is always held regardless of any future failure.

That is, a committing-able output message is always sent once and only once, despite any future process failure.

Theorem 1-1. *In log based rollback recovery, an output message is committing-able if the state interval in which it is sent is recoverable.*

Proof. Under the condition given in the theorem, if any process in the system fails, the state interval in which the output message is sent will be recovered. So, the output message sending event is executed during recovery; it is possible for the processes to avoid sending any message to outside of the world or other processes. That is, despite any process failure, the output message can be sent once and only once. □

By theorem 1-1, if the state interval the output message being sent is always recoverable, the output message can be fast sent to outside of the world, such as in pessimistic message logging. Otherwise, the processes need to coordinate their action to make sure the state interval the message being sent is recoverable. In this case, the coordination between

6

processes may delay the delivery of output message to outside of the world.

Unlike log based rollback recovery, in checkpoint based rollback recovery, the state interval the output message being sent needs to be consistent with the other processes' state. Thus, checkpoint based rollback recovery does not suit for the applications that need frequent interaction with outside of the world.

1.2 Checkpoint based Rollback Recovery

Checkpoint based rollback-recovery is an effective approach to tolerate processes failure. During normal execution, the state of each process saves on stable storage as a local checkpoint. When a failure occurs, the processes in the system are rolled back to the most recent consistent global checkpoint, and are restarted from this state.

There are three categories in checkpoint-based protocols: coordinated checkpointing, uncoordinated checkpointing and communication-induced checkpointing.

1.2.1 Coordinated Checkpointing

Under the Coordinated Checkpointing recovery protocol, processes coordinate their activity to ensure that a consistent global checkpoint is always saved to stable storage in their normal execution. The coordinating action may make processes suffer from high overhead associated with the synchronization messages; and the system performance may degrade due to the blocking of some processes.

There are two approaches to reduce the overhead associated with coordinated checkpoint. The first approach is to minimize the number of synchronization messages [9]; another is to make the process take checkpoint non-blocking [10, 11].

The main advantages of Coordinate Checkpointing protocols are their simplified recovery and not susceptible to the domino effect [12, 13], for each process always restarts from its most recent checkpoint. Additionally, in Coordinated Checkpointing, each process needs to maintain only one checkpoint on stable storage, which may greatly reduce the capacity requirements for stable storage. The garbage collection also becomes very simple, because each process needs only to save a new checkpoint to substitute the old one.

The coordinated activity of processes in taking checkpoint may degrade the performance of process failure free execution, which may be the greatest disadvantage of Coordinate Checkpointing.

1.2.2 Uncoordinated Checkpointing

In Uncoordinated Checkpoint recovery protocols, each process independently takes its checkpoint in its normal execution. If a process fails, it must be rolled back, other processes if their current states causally depend on failed process state also needs to be rolled back to eliminate causal dependencies. This rollback of processes may propagate until all processes are rolled back to the beginning of the computation, which is known as the domino effect.

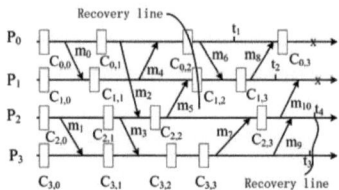

Figure 1.8 Rollback of the processes in the system

For instance, in Figure 1.8, suppose processes p_0 and p_1 fail at "x". To recover from failure, p_0 is rolled back to checkpoint $C_{0,3}$, p_1 is rolled back to $C_{1,3}$. As the state of p_1 at time t_2 records the sending event of m_8 and $C_{0,3}$ records the receipt event of m_8, the state of $C_{0,3}$ causally depends on the state of p_1 at time t_2. When p_1 rolls back to $C_{1,3}$, p_0 needs to be rolled back from $C_{0,3}$ to $C_{0,2}$ to eliminate the causal dependency between the state of $C_{0,3}$ and the state of p_1 at t_2. After p_0 is rolled back to $C_{0,2}$, as the state of p_0 at time t_1 records the sending event of m_6 and $C_{1,3}$ records the receipt event of m_6, p_1 needs to be rolled back to $C_{1,2}$. Finally, all processes are rolled back to the recovery line as shown in Figure 1.8.

In literature, the recovery line [14] is defined as the latest available consistent global checkpoint, which uniquely minimizes the total rollback distance. The recovery line shown in Figure 1.8 is somewhat different from that definition; but it is a consistent global state.

In practice, to recover the failure efficiently, the dependency information can be saved by each process in its normal execution. If failures occur, the failed processes initiate the rollback by broadcasting a dependency request message to collect the dependency information maintained by each process. After receiving the request message, a process stops its execution and sends its dependency information to the sender. Then, the initiator calculates the recovery line on the dependency information received and broadcasts a rollback request message which contains the recovery line. Upon receiving this message, the processes who currently belong to the recovery line simply resume their execution; others roll back to a checkpoint indicated by the recovery line.

There are two methods to calculate the recovery line. One is the *rollback-dependency-graph* [15], another is the *checkpoint-graph* [16], which are all drawn from the dependency information.

The main advantage of Uncoordinated Checkpointing is that a checkpoint can be taken when a process is more convenient, such as in process spare time. So, in process failure free execution, the performance of the system under uncoordinated protocols is better than the performance under coordinated protocols.

There are several disadvantages in Uncoordinated Checkpointing protocols. First, its complex recovery is more difficult to implement than Coordinated Checkpointing. Second, there is the possibility of the domino effect which could possibly cause the system to roll back to the very beginning of the computation. Third, it requires multiple checkpoints of each process to be saved in stable storage. Thus, storage requirement may be large; but some of the checkpoints may be no use because they are not contained in the recovery line.

1.2.3 Communication-Induced Checkpointing

Communication Induced Checkpoint (CIC) tries to take advantage of Uncoordinated and Coordinated Checkpointing. In these protocols, processes take two kinds of checkpoint, local checkpoint and forced checkpoint. CIC protocols do not desire to take a useless checkpoint that will never be part of a consistent global checkpoint. The creation of useless checkpoints is recognized based on the occurrence of specific patterns in which processes communicate and take checkpoints [17]. The CIC protocols recognize potentially dangerous patterns and break them before they occur. This intuition has been formalized in a theory which based on the notion of z-cycles. It has been proved that a checkpoint is useless if and only if it is part of a Z-cycle [18]. Hence, one way to avoid useless checkpoints is to make sure that no Z-path [18] ever becomes a Z-cycle. Enforcing the *no-Z-cycle* condition may require that a process saves additional forced checkpoints in addition to its local checkpoints.

A z-path is a special message sequence that connects two checkpoints.

Given two checkpoints $C_{p,i}$ and $C_{q,j}$, where $C_{x,y}$ denotes the *yth* checkpoint of process x. A Z-path exists between $C_{p,i}$ and $C_{q,j}$ if and only if there are messages $m_1, \ldots m_n$ ($n \geq 1$) such that:

a) m_1 is sent by p after $C_{p,i}$,

b)   If m_k ($1 \leq k \leq n$) is received by the process r, then m_{k+1} is sent by r in the same or a later checkpoint interval, and

c) m_n is received by process q before $C_{q,j}$.

A z-path is a z-cycle if it begins and ends in the same checkpoint interval.

For instance, in Figure 1.9, m_3 is sent by p_0 after $C_{0,1}$ and is received by p_1 before $C_{1,2}$; m_4 is sent by p_1 after $C_{1,2}$ and is received by p_0 before $C_{0,2}$. Thus, there is a z-path $[m_3, C_{1,2}, m_4]$ between $C_{0,1}$ and $C_{0,2}$. Because m_3 and m_4 are sent and received in the same checkpoint interval, $[m_3, C_{1,2}, m_4]$ is also a z- cycle. $C_{1,2}$ is part of a Z-cycle, it is useless checkpoint. In CIC protocols, useless checkpoint should be avoided.

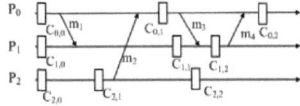

Figure 1.9 A z-cycle: m_3, $C_{1,2}$, m_4

CIC protocols are believed to have several advantages over other styles of rollback-recovery. For instance, they allow processes considerable autonomy in deciding when to take checkpoints. A process can thus take a checkpoint when saving the state would incur a small overhead. CIC protocols are also believed to scale up well with a larger number of processes since they do not require the processes to participate in taking a global checkpoint. But there are costs to pay for these advantages. First, the protocol-specific information piggybacked on messages occasionally "induces" processes to take forced checkpoints before they can process the messages; this may degrade the performance of the system in its normal execution. Second, they also need to keep several checkpoints on stable storage. These advantages and disadvantages are potentially arguable.

1.3 Log based Rollback Recovery

In general, log based rollback recovery [5, 10, 19, 20] uses message logging and checkpoint to provide fault tolerance property for the system. In system normal execution, each message received by a process is recorded in a message log and the state of each process is occasionally saved as a checkpoint. Checkpoints can be taken individually by each process and no coordination is required between the different processes in taking checkpoints. The logged messages and checkpoints are stored in some way that could survive any failures; such as by writing them to a file server in the network.

The recovery of a failed process by the logged messages and checkpoints is based on the assumption that the execution of the process is deterministic between receipt events of message. In other words, if two processes start in the same state and receive the same sequence of messages, they must do the same computation and must finish in the same state. Thus, the state of a process is completely determined by its initial state and by the sequence of message receipt events. If failures occur the failed processes can be recovered by using their checkpoints and the log of messages. First, the state of the failed process is reloaded from the checkpoint onto some available processor. Then, the process is allowed to begin its recovery execution; the sequence of messages logged is replayed to it from the log. These replayed messages must be received by the process in the same order which they were received before the failure. The recovering process re-executes from its checkpoint with the same messages in the same order, and thus deterministically reaches the state it was in after this sequence of messages is originally received. During process re-execution before reaching the maximum recoverable state of the system, a process will re-send some messages that it has sent during its normal execution. These messages are duplicated messages, thus must be detected and ignored by their receivers, or must not be allowed by the system to be transmitted again during recovery.

There are three flavors message logging protocols: pessimistic, optimistic and causal protocols, which each have different failure-free performance, latency of output committing, and simplicity of recovery etc.

1.3.1 *Always-no-orphan* Consistency Condition

In message log based rollback recovery, a process is an orphan process if its state interval depends on a nondeterministic receipt event that cannot be reproduced during recovery. An orphan process must be rolled back even if it does not fail during recovery.

For instance, in Figure 1.10, suppose process p_1 fails at "x" before it logs m_2 to stable storage, and m_1 and m_3 have been logged on stable storage. Apparently, $R(m_2) \rightarrow R(m_3)$, where $\rightarrow$ denotes Lamport's *happen-before relation*, $R(m_2)$ and $R(m_3)$ denote respectively the receipt events of m_2 and m_3. That is, the state interval of p_3 after receiving m_3 depends on $R(m_2)$. Because $R(m_2)$ cannot be reproduced during recovery, p_3 is an orphan process.

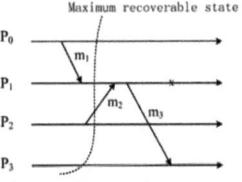

Figure 1.10 An orphan process p_3

A message is said to be stable if its determinant has been logged to stable storage. A stable message can be used in message replaying during recovery.

Let $R(m)$ denote the nondeterministic receipt event of message m, each message m leads to a set $Depend(R(m))$ of processes whose state interval depends on $R(m)$. $Depend(R(m))$ consists of those processes, who receives m, or their state interval depends or causally depends on receipt event of m. For instance, in Figure 1.10, $Depend(R(m_1))=\{p_1\}$, $Depend(R(m_2))=\{p_1,p_3\}$, $Depend(R(m_3))=\{p_3\}$.

Let $log(R(m))$ denote the set of processes that have logged a copy of the determinant of $R(m)$ in their volatile memory not on stable storage. As shown in Figure 1.10, if messages m_1, m_2 and m_3 are only logged in volatile memory of its receiver process, then $log(R(m_1))=\{p_1\}$, $log(R(m_2))=\{p_1\}$, $log(R(m_3))=\{p_3\}$.

The *always-no-orphans* Consistency Condition [7] is expressed as:

$$\forall m: \neg Stable(R(m)) \Rightarrow Depend(R(m)) \subseteq log(R(m))$$

Where $R(m)$ denotes the message receipt event of message m; $Stable(R(m))$ is a predict that is true if the determinant of $R(m)$ is logged on stable storage.

By the condition mentioned above, when failures occur, there are no orphan processes if for each $R(m)$ unlogged on stable storage there are no processes depending on it except for the receiver process of m.

For instance, in Figure 1.10, because $R(m_2)$ is logged in volatile memory not on stable storage, $\neg Stable(R(m_2))$ is true. As $Depend(R(m_2))=\{p_1, p_3\}$, $log(R(m_2))=\{p_1\}$, $Depend(R(m_2))$ is not contained by $log(R(m_2))$; $Depend(R(m_2)) \subseteq log(R(m_2))$ is false. The *always-no-orphans* condition does not hold in such case above. In fact, there is an orphan process p_3 in the system then.

1.3.2 Pessimistic Logging

Pessimistic message logging protocols log the determinant of a message receipt event on stable storage before this event is allowed to affect the computation, which is often referred to as *synchronous logging*. These synchronous logging protocols hold a strengthening *always-no-orphans* condition [2]:

$$\forall m: \neg Stable(R(m)) \Rightarrow |Depend(R(m))| = 0$$

This property stipulates that if a nondeterministic event $R(m)$ has not been saved in stable storage, then there is no process depends on it.

Synchronous logging can potentially degrade the performance of system failure tree execution. To reduce the degradation, some protocol [21] implements the weaker property, which still meets the *always-no-orphans* condition:

11

$$\forall m: \neg Stable(R(m)) \Rightarrow |Depend(R(m))| = 1$$

This property stipulates that the process can defer the logging the determinant of a receipt event on stable storage until it communicates with other processes, such as sending a message to other processes.

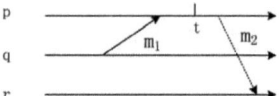

Figure 1.11 Only one process depends on the message receipt event

For instance in Figure 1.11, under the condition above, process p must log the determinant of $R(m_1)$ before it sends message m_2 to process r. Suppose p logs $R(m_1)$ at time t. Thus, before time t, $\neg Stable(R(m_1))$ is true; $|Depend(R(m_1))|=1$ is true, which means only one process p depends on the event of $R(m_1)$. After time t, $\neg Stable(R(m_1))$ is false because the determinant of $R(m_1)$ is logged in stable storage. In both cases, *always-no-orphans condition* is always held.

There are two approaches in pessimistic message logging protocols, i.e., sender-based and receiver-based message logging.

Receiver-based message logging approach [22, 23] logs the determinant of each received message to the stable storage before the message is processed by the application process. Thus, this approach simplifies the recovery of failed processes; its main drawback is the high failure-free overhead caused by synchronous logging.

Sender-based logging approach [23, 24, 25] enables each message to be logged in the volatile memory of its sender to avoid logging messages to stable storage synchronous. The determinant of a message is logged in two steps. First, the sender process logs the content of a message m in its volatile memory before sending it. Second, after this message is received, the receiver process sends an acknowledgement with the receiving order of this message to the sender process, and then the sender adds the receiving order to the determinant. Compared with receiver-based approach, sender-based approach reduces the failure-free overhead of the system because it needs not synchronously log the determinants of message in stable storage.

Pessimistic protocols have the main advantage of being able to just restore the failed processes without affecting the states of other processes not failed.

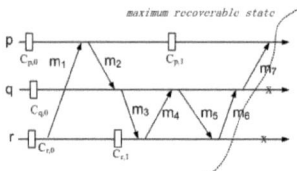

Figure 1.12 Only failed processes rollback

For example, as shown in Figure 1.12, suppose processes q and r fail at "x" respectively. Under pessimistic protocol, the determinants of m_1 to m_7 must be logged in stable storage before the failures occurring. During recovery, only failed processes q and r are rolled back to checkpoint $C_{q,0}$ and $C_{r,1}$ respectively. Then, they replay their receipt events individually. As p does not fail, it needs not be rolled back, it could have just waited for the failed processes recovering from their failures. The maximum recoverable state is just at the time before the failures occur, and after reaching this state the system will begin its normal execution.

In pessimistic protocols, as any message can be replayed, by theorem 1-1, the state interval at which the failure occurs is always recoverable. The output message is also always committing-able at any time. Thus, in pessimistic protocols, the processes can send output messages to outside of the world immediately.

Furthermore, in pessimistic protocols, because the failed process always rolls back to its most recent checkpoint; each process needs only take one checkpoint. This may reduce the capacity requirement for stable storage and simplify the garbage collection.

The main drawback of pessimistic protocol is the high failure-free overhead caused by synchronous logging; this may degrade the performance of the system in its normal execution.

1.3.3 Optimistic Logging

Contrasting to Pessimistic protocols, in Optimistic message logging protocols, the processes log the messages asynchronously to stable storage [5]. After receiving a message, receiver process does not log the determinant of message on stable storage immediately, even if it sends a message to another process. The determinants of messages are kept in a volatile log, from which the determinants are periodically flushed to stable storage.

Optimistic protocols have not implemented the *always-no-orphans* condition, so when failures occur there may be some temporary orphan processes in the system. But, the system requires that the property must be held before the message replaying begins. To hold the property, the orphan processes must roll back to the states do not depend on any message receipt events which cannot be reproduced during recovery.

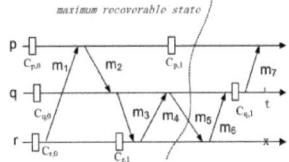

Figure 1.13 Orphan processes p and q rollback

For example, in Figure 1.13, suppose process r fails at "x" before it logs the determinant of m_5. As the state of process q and p depends on or causally depend on the receipt event of m_5, they are all orphan processes. After r being rolled back to checkpoint $C_{r,1}$, process q has also to be rolled back to $C_{q,0}$ not to its most recent checkpoint $C_{q,1}$ to eliminate the dependence relation. Similarly, process p also needs to roll back to checkpoint $C_{p,1}$. During recovery, the system will reach the maximum recoverable state as shown in Figure 1.13, and then begins its normal execution.

To perform rollbacks efficiently, optimistic logging protocols track causal dependencies during processes failure-free execution. Upon a failure, the dependency information is used to calculate the global state in which no process is an orphan and from which the system will be recovered to the maximum recoverable state.

There are two recovery approaches in optimistic protocols: *synchronous* and *asynchronous*.

13

In *synchronous* recovery, there are two kinds of dependency tracking: *direct* and *transitive*. In *direct tracking* [26, 27], the state interval index of sender process is piggybacked on the outgoing message. After receiving a message, the receiver process records the dependency directly caused by this message. At recovery time, the direct dependencies are assembled to obtain complete dependency information which can be used to eliminate the causal dependency among processes. In *transitive tracking*, each process p_i keeps a n-vector TD_i, where $TD[i]$ is p_i's current state interval index, $TD[j]$, $j\neq i$, is the highest state interval index of p_j on which p_i depends. Upon receiving a message with a n-vector V, p_i increments $TD[i]$ by 1, and sets $TD[j]$, $j\neq i$, to the maximum of $TD[j]$ and $V[j]$. At recovery time, the transitive dependencies recorded in the n-vector TD_i can be used to eliminate the causal dependency among processes.

In asynchronous recovery [5], a failed process restarts by sending a rollback announcement broadcast or a recovery message broadcast to start a new incarnation. When receiving a rollback announcement, a process rolls back if it detects that it has become an orphan, and then it broadcasts its own rollback announcement. The rollback will continue until a consistent global state is reached.

Because messages are logged asynchronously, optimistic protocols have the advantage of significantly reducing the overhead caused by message logging relative to pessimistic protocols.

The main drawback of Optimistic message logging is that failure recovery may take longer time to complete, because more processes may have to be rolled back. Because each process may save multiple checkpoints, Optimistic protocols require more space of stable storage than Pessimistic protocols.

1.3.4 Causal Logging

Causal logging protocols [28, 29] have the advantage of Optimistic protocols in failure free execution and remain most of the advantage of Pessimistic protocols. They achieve these goals by using an *antecedence-graph*, uncoordinated checkpoint, and Sender based volatile message logging. The *antecedence-graph* maintained in a process records the *happened-before* relation between certain events in the computation.

Causal logging protocols hold the *always-no-orphans* condition by ensuring that the message receipt event which causally precedes the process state is either stable or available to that process. Each process maintains determinants of non-deterministic event in its volatile log; these determinants are piggybacked on each outgoing message. On receiving a message, the receiver first adds the determinants piggybacked to its volatile determinant log, and then it delivers the message to the application.

Consider the example shown in Figure 1.14, the non-deterministic message receipt events causally precede the state of process p at time t are $R(m_1)$, $R(m_2)$ and $R(m_3)$. In Causal protocols, determinants of these messages must be or stable, or in a volatile log of the process p. If processes q and r fail at "x" respectively, and the receipt events of m_4 and m_5 are not stable, q and r can be recovered under the guidance of p. Although the information about m_4 and m_5 are not available anywhere, but, after receiving m_2 q can deterministically send m_4 to process r, so does m_5. The corresponding maximum recoverable state is shown in Figure 1.14, but it is not same as the pessimistic protocols, the receipt events of m_4 and m_5 are executed in processes normal execution, not in their recovery time.

14

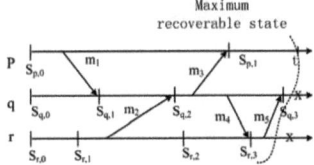

Figure 1.14 q and r recovered under guidance of p

In causal logging, the *antecedence-graph* [29] provides each process with complete information of non-deterministic events which have a causal effect on its state. The causal information in an *antecedence-graph* is propagated in time by the system to renew the old one maintained in each process. For example, the *antecedence-graph* of process p at time t is shown in Figure 1.15 which is drawn from Figure 1.14. Nodes in this graph represent each state interval which precedes the state of process p by the time t, and the edges represent the *happened-before* relation between two state intervals.

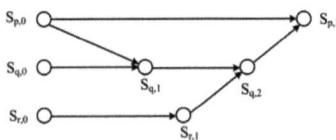

Figure 1.15 Antecedence graph of p at time t

Causal logging avoids synchronous logging recovery information on stable storage most of the time, thereby reducing the overhead in process failure free execution. It also reduces the latency of output commit by allowing messages to be sent to the outside world without multi-host coordination. Upon a failure, surviving processes are not rolled back, and failed processes are rolled back only to their most recent checkpoints.

The main disadvantage of Causal logging may be the overhead caused by piggybacking the information of *antecedence-graph* on a message sent. In practice, to reduce the overhead of the system, each message could carry an *antecedence-graph* that is only a superset of the one piggybacked on previous message sent from this same process.

Chapter 2 Message Number Check Theory

Summary

In this chapter, to study the consistence of the global state of a distributed system, the global state is denoted as a function of time variable or clock variable. The message number sent and received by each process is recorded in U and T matrix such that the study of consistence global state is changed into mathematical issue. Then we propose the message number check theory and methods, in which the consistence of global state, the condition of no orphan messages are all determined by the properties of U and T matrixes.

2.1 Global State Function of Time Variable

We take a distributed system to consist of process p_i, i=1, 2..., n. All the processes in the system do not share a common memory; they are connected by communication channel.

Each process p_i has a local state LS_i which transforms as p_i executes. Mathematically, a global state $G=(LS_1,LS_2,...LS_n)$ is formed by each process local state LS_i of process p_i, i=1,2,... n. This process local state consists of process internal state and channel state [8].

A consistent global state of a distributed system, informally, is the state when simultaneously freezing execution of all participating processes and then recording every process's state [8, 9].

Checkpointing is a technology used to record the local state of each process in stable storage [10]. A local state of a process is called a checkpoint after it is saved in stable storage. A global state of a distributed system is called a global checkpoint if the state of each process in the system is checkpointed.

Though there is no unique clock in distributed systems, the system global state can also be expressed as a function of physical time variable because it also changes with physical time [8]. And from this, we can research the property of global state a distributed system without freezing execution of it.

Definition 2-1. Suppose P_1, P_2, ...P_n are all processes in a system, a distributed systems global state function of physical time variable is denoted as:

$$G(t)=G(LS_1(t),LS_2(t),... LS_n(t)) \qquad (2-1)$$

Where, t denotes physical time variable; $LS_i(t)$ denotes a local state function of process P_i.

As a process local state consists of process internal state and channel state, $LS_i(t)$, i=1, 2... n, can be further denoted as:

$$LS_i(t)= LS_i(P_i(t), CH_i(t)) \qquad (2-2)$$

Where, $P_i(t)$ denotes process P_i's internal state function of t; $CH_i(t)$ denotes process P_i's channel state function of t.

$CH_i(t)$ can be expressed as a composite function of receiving state function $R_i(t)$ and channel sending state function $S_i(t)$:

$$CH_i(t)=CH_i(R_i(t),S_i(t)) \qquad (2-3)$$

Where, $R_i(t)$ denotes P_i's channel receiving state function of t. $S_i(t)$ denotes P_i's channel sending state function of t.

From formula (2-1), (2-2) and (2-3), a volatile consistent distributed system global state function could be

16

expressed as:

$$G(t) = G(LS_1(t), LS_2(t), ...LS_n(t))$$

$$= G(LS_1(P_1(t), CH_1(t)), LS_2(P_2(t), CH_2(t)), ...LS_n(P_n(t), CH_n(t)))$$

$$= G(LS_1(P_1(t), CH_1(R_1(t), S_1(t))), ...LS_n(P_n(t), CH_n(R_n(t), S_n(t)))) \quad (2\text{-}4)$$

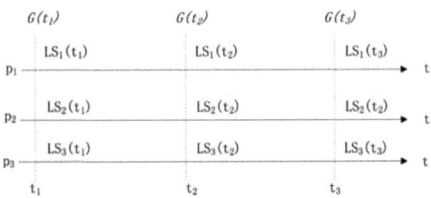

Figure 2.1 Volatile consistent global states at time t_1, t_2 and t_3

For example, suppose a distributed system consists of processes P_1, P_2 and P_3 as shown in Figure 2.1. If time variable t takes values from t_1 to t_3, the corresponding distributed system volatile consistent global states are:

$$G(t_1) = G(LS_1(t_1), LS2(t_1), LS_3(t_1))$$

$$G(t_2) = G(LS_1(t_2), LS_2(t_2), LS_3(t_2))$$

$$G(t_3) = G(LS_1(t_3), LS_2(t_3), LS_3(t_3))$$

In fact, by the notion of consistent global state, at any time t_i, $G(t_i)$ always gives a volatile consistent global state of the system.

2.2 Global State Function of Clock Variable

Mostly, each process of the distributed system executes on itself computer and the working of each computer is driven by its system clock. To find out a consistent global state among many local process states, maybe it is useful to express the system global state as a function of processor clock [8] variable. That is, the system global state may be composed of each process local state at a time which is different from other processes.

Definition 2-2. Suppose P_1, P_2 ... P_i ... P_n are all processes in a distributed system, a distributed system global state function of processor clock variable is denoted as:

$$G(c_1, c_2...c_n)$$

$$= G(LS_1(c_1), ...LS_n(c_n))$$

$$= G(LS_1(P_1(c_1), CH_1(c_1)), LS_2(P_2(c_2), CH_2(c_2)), ...LS_n(P_n(c_n), CH_n(c_n))) \quad (2\text{-}5)$$

Where, c_i denotes processor clock variable of P_i, i= 1, 2,... n. And, c_i does not relate to another processor clock variable. $LS_i(c_i)$ denotes process P_i local state function of c_i. $P_i(c_i)$ denotes process P_i internal state function of c_i. $CH_i(c_i)$ denotes process P_i channel state function of c_i, which can also be expressed as a composite function of $R_i(c_i)$ and $S_i(c_i)$: $CH_i(c_i) = CH_i(R_i(c_i), S_i(c_i))$.

In fact, the processor clock c_i of P_i is correlative to others, for the system will synchronize the processor clock with an authoritative external source time [8]. But, when we study consistency of global state from several process local states, it is useful to suppose that processor clock is independent to others and each processor clock variable can take any value.

From formula (2-5), if the processor variable c_i takes value of t_i, i=1, 2...n; and then distributed systems volatile global state can be expressed as:

$G(t_1, t_2, ...t_n)$

$= G(LS_1(t_1), ...LS_n(t_n))$

$= G(LS_1(P_1(t_1), CH_1(t_1)), ...LS_n(P_n(t_n), CH_n(t_n)))$ (2-6)

As t_i may be any value of clock variable c_i, the global state $G(t_1, t_2, ... t_n)$ may be consistent or not, which depends on the values of all t_i, i=1, 2... n.

2.3 Message Number Check Theory

Under some condition, the consistency of global checkpoint can be determined by the message number of each process sent and received. This sub-chapter will focus on the properties of message number of distributed systems.

The definitions and theorems in this sub-chapter are all under the assumption that distributed system consists of process $P_1, P_2...P_n$, and communication subsystem receives message reliably, in FIFO (First Input First Output) order.

Under the assumption of a *FIFO* reliable communication subsystem, the system global state may possess some unknown property which relates to the number of messages received and sent by processes. For example, in Figure 2.2, $G(t_5,t_3,t_2)$ is a consistent global state, because in this state the number of message sent by any process is always greater than the number of message received by corresponding receiver. While, $G(t_5,t_4,t_1)$ is not a consistent global state, actually the number of messages sent to q by r is less than the number of messages received by q from r.

To study the relation of the consistency of global state and the number of messages sent and received by processes, we define data structures of T and U [30] matrix in the follow paragraph.

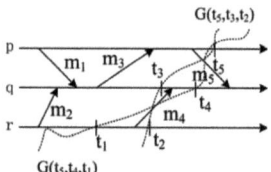

Figure 2.2 Consistency of global state determined by message number

As the T and U matrix may change with the time, they are functions of the time variables. For ease of expression, we use superscript to denote the time value of the T and U matrix and its components in the following chapter. For instance, $T^{(t1,t2...tn)}$ denotes $T(t_1,t_2...t_n)$, $T_i^{(ti)}$ denotes $T_i(t_i)$, $T_{ij}^{(ti)}$ denotes $T_{ij}(t_i)$.

Definition 2-3. The improved vector logical clock $T_i^{(ti)}$ of process P_i is defined as:

$T_i^{(ti)}=[T_{i1}^{(ti)}, ...T_{ii}^{(ti)}, ...T_{in}^{(ti)}]$, i=1,2,...n. (2-7)

Where, $T_{ii}^{(ti)}$ denotes the number of message sent by P_i by the time t_i, its initial value is zero, $T_{ii}^{(ti)}$ adds 1 after a message is sent by P_i. $T_{im}^{(ti)}$, i≠m, m=1, 2...n, denotes the number of messages P_i received from process P_m by the time t_i. t_i is the value of c_i which denotes P_i's processor clock variable.

18

The improved vectors $T_1^{(t1)}$, $T_2^{(t2)}$…$T_n^{(tn)}$ corresponding to processes $P_1,P_2…P_n$ respectively construct a T matrix, as shown in Figure 2.3.

In Figure 2.3, diagonal elements $T_{ii}^{(ti)}$ corresponding to the process P_i records the number of messages sent by P_i to all other processes in the system. $T_{im}^{(ti)}$ ($m\neq i$,) records the number of messages P_i received from P_m.

$$T^{(t1,t2…tn)} = \begin{bmatrix} T_1^{(t1)} \\ T_2^{(t2)} \\ … \\ T_n^{(tn)} \end{bmatrix} = \begin{bmatrix} T_{11}^{(t1)}\ T_{12}^{(t1)}…T_{1n}^{(t1)} \\ T_{21}^{(t2)}T_{22}^{(t2)}…T_{2n}^{(t2)} \\ …. \\ T_{n1}^{(tn)}T_{n2}^{(tn)}…T_{nn}^{(tn)} \end{bmatrix}$$

Figure 2.3 T matrix of the distributed system

An example of improved vector logical clock of a system is shown in Figure 2.4. For process p, the initial value of the improved vector logical clock is [0, 0, 0]. At time t_2, it sends a message m_1 to process q, so $T_p^{(t2)}$=[1,0,0]. After receiving m_3 from q, $T_p^{(t7)}$=[1,1,0]. $T_p^{(t9)}$=[2,1,0], after it sends m_5 to q. Accordingly, $T_q^{(t3)}$=[0,0,1], $T_q^{(t4)}$=[1,0,1], $T_q^{(t5)}$=[1,1,1], $T_q^{(t8)}$=[1,1,2], $T_q^{(t10)}$=[2,1,2]; $T_r^{(t1)}$=[0,0,1], $T_r^{(t6)}$=[0,0,2].

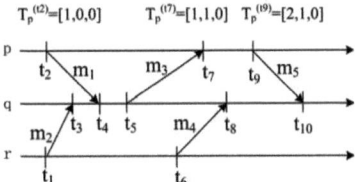

Figure 2.4 Improved vector logical clocks of a system

The T matrix of the system in Figure 2.4 can be combined by improved vector logical clocks of each process. For example, $T^{(t7,t5,t6)}$ can be combined by $T_p^{(t7)}$=[1,1,0], $T_q^{(t5)}$=[1,1,1] and $T_r^{(t6)}$=[0,0,2], as shown in Figure 2.5.

$$T^{(t7,t5,t6)} = \begin{bmatrix} 1 & 1 & 0 \\ 1 & 1 & 1 \\ 0 & 0 & 2 \end{bmatrix}$$

Fig.2-5. A T matrix of a system

Definition 2-4. The sending vector $U_i^{(ti)}$ of process P_i is defined as:

$$U_i^{(ti)}=[U_{i1}^{(ti)}…U_{ii}^{(ti)}…U_{in}^{(ti)}]\ ,\ i=1,2,…n. \tag{2-8}$$

Where, $U_{ii}^{(ti)}$ always equals zero; $U_{im}^{(ti)}$, $m\neq i$, m=1, 2,…n, denotes the number of messages P_i sent to P_m by the time t_i.

$$U^{(t1,t2…tn)} = \begin{bmatrix} U_1^{(t1)} \\ U_2^{(t2)} \\ … \\ U_n^{(tn)} \end{bmatrix} = \begin{bmatrix} U_{11}^{(t1)}\ U_{12}^{(t1)}…U_{1n}^{(t1)} \\ U_{21}^{(t2)}U_{22}^{(t2)}…U_{2n}^{(t2)} \\ …. \\ U_{n1}^{(tn)}U_{n2}^{(tn)}…U_{nn}^{(tn)} \end{bmatrix}$$

Figure 2.6 U matrix of the distributed system

The sending vectors $U_1^{(t1)}$, $U_2^{(t2)}$…$U_n^{(tn)}$ corresponding to process $P_1,P_2,…P_n$ respectively, construct a U matrix, as shown in Figure 2.6.

In Figure 2.6, the diagonal elements $U_{ii}^{(ti)}$ is always zero, $U_{im}^{(ti)}$ ($i \neq m$) records the number of messages P_i sent to P_m by the time t_i.

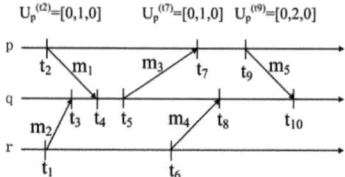

Figure 2.7 Sending vectors of a system

An example of sending vector of a system is shown in Figure 2.7. For process p, the initial value of the vector is [0, 0, 0]. After p sends m_1 to q, $U_p^{(t2)} = [0,1,0]$. $U_p^{(t9)} = [0,2,0]$, after p sends m_5 to q. Accordingly, $U_q^{(t5)} = [1,0,0]$, $U_r^{(t1)} = [0,1,0]$, $U_r^{(t6)} = [0,2,0]$.

The U matrix of the system in Figure 2.7 can be combined by the sending vector of each process. For example, $U^{(t9,t5,t6)}$ can be combined by $U_p^{(t9)} = [0,2,0]$, $U_q^{(t5)} = [1,0,0]$ and $U_r^{(t6)} = [0,2,0]$, as shown in Figure 2.8.

$$U^{(t7,t5,t6)} = \begin{bmatrix} 0 & 2 & 0 \\ 1 & 0 & 0 \\ 0 & 2 & 0 \end{bmatrix}$$

Figure 2.8 A U matrix of a system

An orphan message m corresponding to a global checkpoint has such property that its receiving event is recorded in the global checkpoint, but the corresponding sending event is not.

Theorem 2-1. *Suppose a distributed system consists of $p_1, p_2 \ldots p_n$. There must be some orphan messages in a global checkpoint $G(t_1, t_2, \ldots t_n)$, iff $\exists i, m; i, m \in \{ 1, 2 \ldots n \}$, $U_{im}^{(ti)} < T_{mi}^{(tm)}$. Where, t_i, $i=1,2 \ldots n$, denotes the time by which the local process state of p_i is checkpointed.*

Proof of sufficiency (if part): By the postulation of the theorem, the number of messages process P_i sent to P_m is fewer than the number of messages P_m received from P_i. There must be some messages that their receiving events have been recorded by P_m by the time t_m, but their sending events have not been recorded by P_i by the time t_i. So, there must be some orphan messages in $G(t_1, t_2, \ldots t_n)$.

Proof of necessity (only if part): suppose there are some orphan messages in $G(t_1, t_2, \ldots t_n)$, thus there must be some messages that their receiving events have been recorded by some processes, but their sending events have not been recorded by any processes in the system. That is, $\exists$ i, m; the receipt events of some messages P_i sent to P_m are recorded by P_m by the time t_m, the sending events of these messages is not recorded by P_i by the time t_i. So the number of messages P_i sent to P_m is fewer than the number of messages P_m received from P_i, that is $U_{im}^{(ti)} < T_{mi}^{(tm)}$. □

20

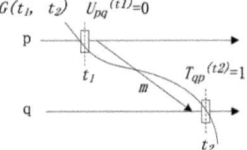

Figure 2.9 An orphan message in $G(t_1, t_2)$

For example, as shown in Figure 2.9, p has not send m to q by the time t_1, $U_{pq}^{(t1)}=0$; q receives m by the time t_2, $T_{qp}^{(t2)}=1$, $U_{pq}^{(t1)} < T_{qp}^{(t2)}$, there is an orphan message m in global state $G(t_1, t_2)$.

A global checkpoint is consistent if there is no orphan message in it [15]. A global checkpoint is strongly consistent if there is no orphan message and in-transit message in it [12].

Theorem 2-2. $\forall i, i \in \{1, 2,...n\}$, $\forall m, m \in \{1, 2,...n\}$, $i \neq m$;

If $U_{im}^{(ti)} > T_{mi}^{(tm)}$, then the global state $G(t_1, t_2...t_n)$ is a consistent one and there must be some in-transit messages in $G(t_1,... t_i...t_m ...t_n)[30]$;

if $U_{im}^{(ti)} = T_{mi}^{(tm)}$, then $G(t_1, t_2...t_n)$ is a strong consistent global state.

Proof.

Case one, if $\forall i$, $\forall m$, $U_{im}^{(ti)} > T_{mi}^{(tm)}$, there must be no message which its receipt event has been recorded in $G(t_1,... t_i...t_m ...t_n)$ and its sending event has not. By the notion of consistency of global state, $G(t_1, t_2... t_n)$ is a consistent one. As $U_{im}^{(ti)}$ is more than $T_{mi}^{(tm)}$, there must be some messages have not been received, so there must be some in-transit messages in $G(t_1,... t_i...t_m ...t_n)$ such that $U_{im}^{(ti)} > T_{mi}^{(tm)}$.

Case two, if $\forall i$, $\forall m$, $U_{im}^{(ti)}=T_{mi}^{(tm)}$, then all messages sent by any process must have been received by other processes. There is no orphan message and in-transit message in $G(t_1,t_2...t_n)$, so $G(t_1,t_2...t_n)$ is a strong consistent global state. □

Theorem 2-3. $\forall i, i \in \{1, 2... n\}$

If, $T_{ii}^{(ti)} > \sum_{j \neq i, j=1,2...n} T_{ji}^{(tj)}$, the global state $G(t_1, t_2...t_n)$ is a consistent global state and there must be some in-transit messages in $G(t_1,... t_i...t_m ...t_n)$;

if $T_{ii}^{(ti)} = \sum_{j \neq i, j=1,2...n} T_{ji}^{(tj)}$, the global state $G(t_1, t_2...t_n)$ is a strong consistent global state.

Proof.

Case one, $\forall i$, $T_{ii}^{(ti)} > \sum_{j \neq i, j=1,2...n} T_{ji}^{(tj)}$. By this condition, all messages sent by any process have been received by other processes, so there are no orphan messages in $G(t_1, t_2...t_n)$. By the notion of consistent global state, $G(t_1, t_2...t_n)$ is a consistent global state. In this case, there must be some in-transit messages in $G(t_1,... t_i...t_m ...t_n)$ such that $T_{ii}^{(ti)} > \sum_{j \neq i, j=1,2...n} T_{ji}^{(tj)}$.

Case two, $\forall i$, $T_{ii}^{(ti)} = \sum_{j \neq i, j=1,2...n} T_{ji}^{(tj)}$, By this condition, all messages sent by any process have been received by other processes, and there are no in-transit messages in $G(t_1,... t_i...t_m ...t_n)$, so $G(t_1,... t_i...t_m ...t_n)$ is a strong consistent

21

global state. □

An example of vector logic clock and sending vector of a system is shown in Figure 2.10. In this Figure, $T_{pp}^{(17)} = 2$, $T_{qp}^{(18)} = 2$, $T_{rp}^{(15)} = 0$, $T_{pp}^{(17)} = T_{qp}^{(18)} + T_{rp}^{(15)}$; $T_{qq}^{(18)} = 1$, $T_{pq}^{(17)} = 0$, $T_{rq}^{(15)} = 1$, $T_{qq}^{(18)} = T_{pq}^{(17)} + T_{rq}^{(15)}$; $T_{rr}^{(15)} = 1$, $T_{pr}^{(17)} = 0$, $T_{qr}^{(18)} = 1$, $T_{rr}^{(15)} = T_{pr}^{(17)} + T_{qr}^{(18)}$. By theorem 2-3, $G(t_7, t_8, t_5)$ is a strong consistent global state. But, $G(t_2, t_8, t_5)$ is not a consistent global state, for $T_{pp}^{(2)} = 1$, $T_{qp}^{(18)} = 2$, $T_{rp}^{(15)} = 0$, $T_{pp}^{(2)} < T_{qp}^{(18)} + T_{rp}^{(15)}$, in fact there is an orphan message m_4 in $G(t_2, t_8, t_5)$. Accordingly, the same conclusion above can also be deduced by theorem 2-2, to save space we omit it.

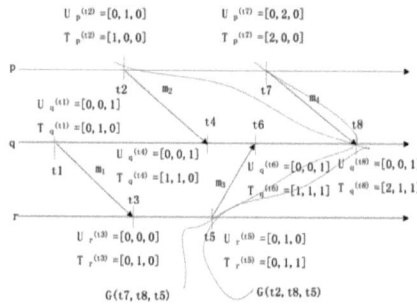

Figure 2.10 Vector logic clock and sending vector of a system

Theorem 2-1, 2-2 and 2-3 are all under the assumption of a reliable FIFO communication subsystem, if there are duplicated messages and out of order messages in the system something will be wrong. For example, in Figure 2.11, $U_{pq}^{(t1)} = 1$, $T_{qp}^{(t2)} = 1$, $U_{pq}^{(t1)} = T_{qp}^{(t2)}$; $U_{qp}^{(t2)} = 0$, $T_{pq}^{(t1)} = 0$, $U_{qp}^{(t2)} = T_{pq}^{(t1)}$; but $G(t_1, t_2)$ is not a consistent one, in fact, there is an orphan message m_2 in $G(t_1, t_2)$.

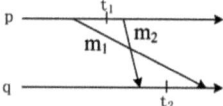

Figure 2.11 A system with Non-FIFO channel

This chapter proposes some simple methods to determine the consistency of global checkpoints. That is, by checking the number of messages sent and received to determine if a global checkpoint is consistent or if there are some in-transit messages or orphan messages in a global checkpoint. These methods will be used in chapter 4 to simplify the design of protocols.

Definition 3-2. The improved logic clock LC_p of process p is an integer variable to record the order of message receiving and sending events such that [35, 36]:

1. The initial value of LC_p is zero.

2. After p sends a message, LC_p increase one.

3. After receiving a message from q, $LC_p \leftarrow max(LC_p+1, LC_q+1)$, where *max* gives improved logic clock with higher value.

As the value of LC_p changes with the message sending and receipt events, so it is a function of these events. Let $LC_p(e)$ denote the improved logic clock function of receipt or sending event e of the process p. Thus, the value of LC_p after p received or sent message m can be denoted as $LC_p((R(m))$ or $LC_p((S(m))$ respectively, where $R(m)$ and $S(m)$ respectively denote the receipt and sending events of m.

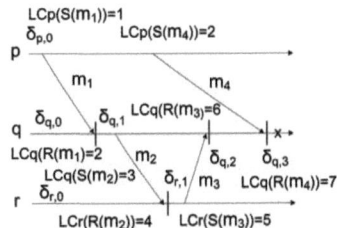

Figure 3.4 Improved logic clocks of p, q, r

For example, as shown in Figure 3.4, let LC_p, LC_q and LC_r denote improved logic clock of process p, q and r, respectively. $LC_q(R(m_1))=2$, after q receives m_1. $LC_q(S(m_2))=3$, after q sends m_2. After receiving m_3 from r, $LC_q(R(m_3))=6$. $LC_q(R(m_4))=7$, after q received m_4. In this case, the order of the message to be replayed is m_1, m_3, m_4 uniquely determined by LC_q's value 2, 6, 7. But, if q fails at "x" and q fails to log determinants of m_1, m_3, m_4 before failure, the volatile value of LC_q is lost because of q's failure. Thus, the order of m_1, m_3 and m_4 cannot be determined by LC_q then.

From the instance above, apparently, the order of message in a sequence cannot be determined by the logic clock of message receiver, for the volatile memory of receiver is lost because of its failure. So, we have to find an alternative variable to replace logic clock of a receiver process.

Theorem 3-2. *If PWD assumption holds and $R(m_i) \xrightarrow{AHB} R(m_j)$, then $LC_p(S(m_i)) < LC_q(S(m_j))$[35, 36].*

Where, $R(m_i)$ and $R(m_j)$ denote the receipt events of m_i and m_j of process k respectively. $LC_p(S(m_i))$ denotes the value of logic clock of process p after the message m_i is sent to process k. $LC_q(S(m_j))$ denotes the value of logic clock of process q after message m_j is sent to process k.

Proof. As $R(m_i) \xrightarrow{AHB} R(m_j)$, $R(m_j)$ logically depends on $R(m_i)$, $S(m_j)$ is a deterministic event; so $R(m_i) \xrightarrow{AHB} S(m_j)$. Otherwise, suppose $R(m_i)$ does not always happen before $S(m_j)$, this means $R(m_i)$ and $S(m_j)$ may occur in any order; or $R(m_i)$ precedes $S(m_j)$, or $S(m_j)$ precedes $R(m_i)$. Suppose $S(m_j)$ occurs before $R(m_i)$, that is $S(m_j) \rightarrow R(m_i)$. As $S(m_j) \rightarrow R(m_j)$, $S(m_j)$ directly occurs before $R(m_j)$, so $S(m_j)$ only precedes $R(m_i)$ indirectly. That is, as shown in Figure 3.5, there must be at least one message m_k between m_j and m_i, such that $S(m_j) \rightarrow S(m_k)$, $S(m_k) \rightarrow R(m_k)$, $R(m_k) \rightarrow S(m_i)$, $S(m_i)$

$\rightarrow R(m_i)$. In such case, m_j and m_i must be transited in different paths which having a different channel delay. Thus $R(m_i)$ cannot always happen before $R(m_j)$, because this contradicts to the theorem postulation. So $R(m_i) \xrightarrow{AHB} S(m_j)$. According to definition 3-2, the value of $LC_p(R(m_i))$ must be fewer than the value of $LC_q(S(m_j))$; that is, $LC_p(R(m_i)) < LC_q(S(m_j))$. As $S(m_i) \xrightarrow{AHB} R(m_i)$, $LC_p(S(m_i)) < LC_p(R(m_i))$. So, $LC_p(S(m_i)) < LC_p(R(m_i)) < LC_q(S(m_j))$, $LC_p(S(m_i)) < LC_q(S(m_j))$. □

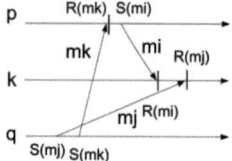

Figure 3.5 $S(m_j)$ indirectly precedes $R(m_i)$

As shown in Figure 3.6, if $R(m_i)$ always happens before $R(m_j)$, then $LC_p(S(m_i)) < LC_q(S(m_j))$; otherwise $LC_p(S(m_i))$ may be greater than $LC_q(S(m_j))$, or equal to $LC_q(S(m_j))$. But if a message receipt order is determined by the logic clock of the message sender, then at least the *always-happens-before* relation between any receipt events can be always held. So, it is good idea to rearrange a message sequence by the logic clock of the message sender for the message replaying in the recovery.

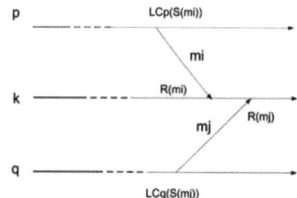

Figure 3.6 Receipt order determined by sender's logic clock

As an example of message rearranging as shown in Figure 3.4, suppose q fails at "x". The message sequence to be replayed should have been m_1, m_3 and m_4. As $R(m_1) \xrightarrow{AHB} R(m_3)$, $R(m_1) \xrightarrow{AHB} R(m_4)$, $R(m_3) \xrightarrow{NAHB} R(m_4)$, $R(m_4) \xrightarrow{NAHB} R(m_3)$, the message sequence m_1, m_4, m_3 is equivalent to message sequence m_1, m_3, m_4. Let $<LC_x(S(m)), m>$ denote a tuple which consists of the message m and the sender process x logic clock $LC_x(S(m))$. According to theorem 3-2, the message receipt order in an equivalent sequence can be determined by LC_x. That is, the message receipt order can be rearranged by the sender process logic clock. In Figure 3.4, the tuples corresponding to m_1, m_3 and m_4 are $<LC_p(S(m_1))=1, m_1>$, $<LC_r(S(m_3))=5, m_3>$, $<LC_p(S(m_4))=2, m_4>$. The message sequence rearranged with sender process logic clock is m_1, m_4, m_3 in which the receipt order of messages is only determined by the value of the corresponding logic clock.

Let LC denotes the improved logic clock vector maintained in each process p_i. $LC=[LC_1, LC_2...LC_n]$, where, LC_k, k=i, denotes the improved logic clock of p_i, LC_k, k≠i, denotes p_k's logic clock which p_i knows, n is the number of processes in the system.

If process p fails, then the current LC must be lost if it is not saved to stable storage then. In the following chapter, a method will be proposed to recover the current lost logic clock vector of a process because of its failure.

Suppose each process p_i logs a tuple $< i, j, LC_i(S(m)), m>$ on message log when p_i sends a message m to p_j. That is, when p_i sends a message, $LC_i(S(m)) \leftarrow LC_i(S(m))+1$, logs the tuple, then p_i sends message. And, after receiving message m p_i saves or updates (if $LC_i(R(m))$ has been saved, then updates it) $LC_i(R(m))$ on stable storage before it receives another message.

Theorem 3-3. *Under the assumption above, if a process p_i fails, its volatile current LC must be lost, and then the current LC can be recovered by the information saved in message log and stable storage.*

Proof.

First, we prove that LC_i of LC can be recovered by the information saved in message log and stable storage. If p_i fails, there are two kinds of events may occur before p_i's failure, one kind of event is a message sending event, another is a message receipt event.

Case one, suppose p_i sends a message to another process before its failure, as shown in Figure 3.7 (a). In this case, p_i must have logged $<i, v, LC_i(S(m)), m>$ on the message log. So, LC_i can be recovered from $LC_i(S(m))$ in the message log.

Case two, suppose p_i receives a message m from another process before its failure. In this case, $LC_i(R(m))$ may be saved to stable storage before the failure occurs, or $LC_i(R(m))$ may be lost because of p_i's failure.

Suppose $LC_i(R(m))$ is saved to stable storage, thus LC_i can be recovered from the stable storage as shown in Figure 3.7 (b).

Suppose $LC_i(R(m))$ is not saved to stable storage, there are two cases before p_i receives m. One case is that p_i sends at least one message before it receives m. In this case, as shown in Figure 3.7 (c), after p_i sends m_u to p_w, the tuple $<i, w, LC_i(S(m_u)), m_u>$ must have been logged in the message log. And, before p_v sends m to p_i, the tuple $<v, i, LC_v(S(m)), m>$ must have been logged in the message log. Thus, LC_i can be calculated by the formula: $LC_i \leftarrow max(LC_i(S(m_u))+1, LC_v(S(m))+1)$. Another case is that p_i does not send any message during two message receipt events, as shown in Figure 3.7 (d). In this case, $LC_v(S(m))$ and $LC_i(R(m_k))$ must have been saved on message log and stable storage respectively. Thus, LC_i can be calculated by the formula: $LC_i \leftarrow max(LC_i(R(m_k))+1, LC_v(S(m))+1)$.

Second, we prove that other elements LC_j, $j \neq i$, can be recovered by the information on the message log. Because such elements $<j, i, LC_j, m>$ in message log recorded the information of message p_j sent to p_i, the message with maximum LC_j in the message log must be the last message p_j sent to p_i. So, the current LC_j of LC can be obtained from the element with maximum LC_j among such elements $<j, i, LC_j, m>$ in the message log. □

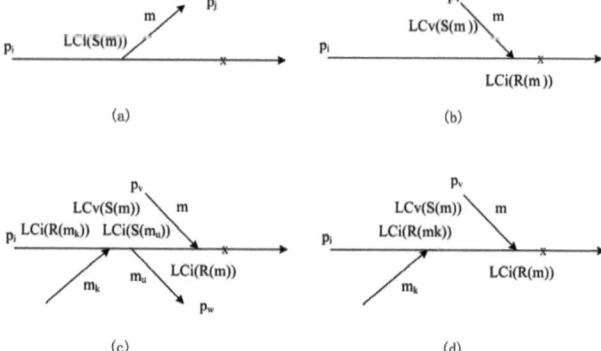

Figure 3.7 *LC* is recovered from the information in stable storage

From theorem 3-3, LC_j, $j \neq i$, of LC in p_i can be simply and accurately recovered during recovery, but LC_i of p_i is more complex to recover. A simple method to recover LC_i is to set it the value which is more than its current value. That is, LC_i can be calculated from the formula: $LC_i \leftarrow \max(LC_i(R(m))+1, LC_{max}+1)$, where $LC_i(R(m))$ is the logic clock most recently saved on stable storage by p_i, LC_{max} is the maximum logic clock value recorded in the message log. In this case, the value of LC_i may be more than its current value which just before failure occurs. But, this LC_i can also be used to rearrange the future message sequence without affecting the previous message sequence to be rearranged upon failures.

Another method to recover LC of process p_i upon failure is to save LC with a checkpoint in stable storage. Thus, upon failure, p_i is rolled back to this checkpoint and the volatile LC can be set to the initial value from LC in stable storage. During message replaying of p_i, as p_i must receive messages from the recovery manager and it may wish to send messages to other processes, thus each element of LC can be updated after each message delivery. Though p_i cannot send a message to a failed process during its recovery, it can only update LC vector without sending any message when it wish to send a message to the failed process. Thus, when p_i is recovered from failure, the LC vector can also be changed to the value just as failure before.

In this chapter, to address the problem which the message receipt order is lost because of failure, we introduce the message rearranging theories and methods, and propose a new theorem to perfect this theory. By these theories and methods, the message receipt order can be calculated from the message sending logic clock. Furthermore, the logic clock vector can be recovered by the information saved in stable storage, thus the message receiver process can deliver the message immediately unlike pessimistic protocols. So, it is possible to design a new protocol to have the merits of pessimistic and optimistic protocols simultaneously.

Chapter 4 Corresponding Protocol

Summary

As examples of message rearranging and message number check theory and method, this chapter proposes a message logging protocol [35, 36] and an algorithm to calculate the recovery line which can be used in uncoordinated checkpoint. Benefit from the new theory and methods, the protocol and algorithm have gotten many advantages than previous ones, and abandoned some drawback of them.

4.1 A Protocol based on Message Rearrange

4.1.1 Introduction

In previous message logging protocols, it is default that the message receipt order cannot be recovered if it is lost. Thus, there evolve Pessimistic, Optimistic and Causal logging to treat the problem of message receipt order loss. After the message rearranging theory and methods are proposed, it is possible to design a new message logging protocol to optimize the rollback recovery. In this new protocol, when process p_i sends message m to p_j, it logs tuple $<i, j, LC_i (S (m)), m>$ on the message log. After receiving a message m, the receiver process p_j delivers m to the applications immediately. The logic clock vector LC of a failed process can be recovered by the methods mentioned in chapter 3. Thus, in this new protocol, processes can act as the processes in optimistic protocol in their normal execution, and meanwhile have the simplified recovery when failure occurs.

4.1.2 System Model

A distributed system is a set of processes, which consists of P_1, P_2...P_n. P_i, i=1, 2...n, do not share a common memory. The communication subsystem receives messages reliably and in FIFO order. Each of the messages is received after an arbitrary finite delay. This protocol satisfies the piecewise deterministic (PWD) model. The message logging protocol tolerates an arbitrary number of fail-stop failures. If a failure occurs, it can be detected by other processes in the system. Our logging protocol adopts optimistic sender-based message logging protocols. Normal processes and recovery processes are two kinds of processes in the distributed system. And each normal process P_i, has a corresponding recovery process denoted as RP_i.

If a failed process wishes to send a message to another failed process, it can only update corresponding data structure without sending any messages.

4.1.3 Main Data Structure

We use T_{ij} to record the total number of the logged messages P_i received from P_j, where i, j =1, 2,... n, i≠ j. U_{ji} records the total number of messages P_j sent to P_i, where i, j =1, 2,... n, i≠ j. T_{ij} is saved with a checkpoint in stable storage when a checkpoint is taken, but it is not saved in stable storage when P_i receives a message from another process. U_{ji} is saved in stable storage, when P_j sends message to another process. If P_i fails, T_{ij} can be recovered from stable storage,

31

and $(U_{ji} - T_{ij})$ can be used to obtain the total numbers of messages received by P_i since its checkpoint is set up.

Each process P_i maintains a n-vector $LC=[LC_1, LC_2,...LC_n]$ in its volatile memory, where LC_k is the improved logic clock of process P_k, k=1,2,... n, n is the number of processes in the system.

Each process P_i also maintains a fault flag n-vector $F= [F_1, F_2,... F_n]$, F_k is set to 1 if P_k is detected a failure and it has not been recovered.

4.1.4 Description of the Protocol

During failure free execution, each process P_i takes its checkpoint independently, including T_i and LC. The old checkpoint is deleted after a new checkpoint is set up.

When P_i sends a message m to P_j, if P_j fails (F_j=1), and P_i does not fail, P_i will wait until P_j is recovered from failure. Otherwise, $LC_i \leftarrow LC_i+1$, save the tuple <i, j, LC_i, m > on the message log in local stable storage, $U_{ij} \leftarrow U_{ij}+1$, save U_i to stable storage, then P_i sends AM<i, LC_i, m> to P_j.

If P_i receives an application message AM<j, LC_j, m> in its normal execution, this message can be sent by P_j or by RP_j. If AM.LC_j > LC_j, where LC_j is the history improved clock, this message must be sent by P_j during failure free execution. So P_i delivers it and updates T_{ij}, LC_j, and LC_i. If AM.$LC_j \leq LC_j$, it is impossible in failure-free process execution of P_j. Because AM.LC_j denotes current logic clock of P_j and LC_j denotes the history of logic clock of P_j, AM.LC_j cannot be less than LC_j. So, this AM must be sent by process P_j in its recovery execution, as this AM has been delivered by P_i, thus P_i discards it.

Upon failure, RP_i loads T_i and LC from checkpoint. Then RP_i broadcasts a message with T_i to RP_k and a message with F_i (with value 1) to P_k respectively, where $T_i= \{T_{i1}, T_{i2}...T_{in}\}$. When receiving messages with T_i, each process RP_k re-sends messages to RP_i, which have been sent to P_i by P_k in normal execution. After receiving all the messages sent by RP_k, RP_i rearranges these messages by their logical clock. Then RP_i loads LC of P_i from stable storage, rolls back P_i to its checkpoint, and then sends this LC to P_i to serve as the initial value of its logic clock vector. After then, RP_i sends the rearranged messages to P_i. P_i replays these rearranged messages then. Afterwards, RP_i broadcasts a message piggyback F_i (with value 0) which means P_i has been recovered.

The main algorithm of RP_i and RP_k is shown below.

RP_i:

    load T_i from checkpoint;

    broadcast message with T_i to RP_k

    broadcast message with F_i (F_i = 1) to P_k

    after receiving all messages with M (source=P_k, dest=P_i, LC_k)

        rearrange M by LC_k in nondecreasing order

        load LC from stable storage

        roll back P_i to its checkpoint, sends LC to P_i

        send rearranged messages to P_i

    broadcast message with F_i (F_i = 0) to P_k

RP_k:

when receiving message with T_i

    load U_{ki} from stable storage;

    diff $\leftarrow U_{ki} - T_{ik}$

    While diff > 0

        Find a logged message M: <k, i , LC_k,m>

        send message M to RP_i.

        diff $\leftarrow$ diff $- 1$

    send END message to RP_i to end this message delivery

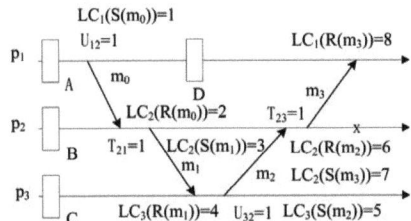

Figure 4.1 An example of our protocol

An example of our recovery protocol is shown in Figure 4.1. Suppose q fails at "x", the elements of 3-vector U_1, U_2, U_3, T_1, T_2, T_3 are all set to zero, and T_1, T_2 and T_3 are saved with checkpoint A, B and C respectively. LC=[0,0,0], is also saved with A, B and C respectively. After sending m_0 to p_2, p_1 save U_1 with U_{12} =1 to stable storage and log m_0 on message log, as shown in Figure 4.2. After the new checkpoint D is set up, p_1 deletes the old checkpoint A. After sending m_1 to p_3, p_2 log m_1 in the message log. After sending m_2 to p_2, p_3 save U_3 with U_{32} =1 to stable storage and log m_2 on the message log. After sending m_3 to p_1, p_2 logs m_3 on the message log. The current logic clock vectors of each process are LC=[8,7,0], LC=[1,7,5], LC=[0,3,5] corresponding to p_1, p_2 and p_3 respectively.

i (S)	j (R)	LCi	m
1	2	1	m0
2	3	3	m1
3	2	5	m2
2	1	7	m3

Figure 4.2 Message log of the system

Upon p_2's failure, the recovery process RP_2 loads T_2 =[0,0,0] and LC=[0,0,0] from checkpoint B. Then RP_2 broadcast T_2 to RP_1 and RP_3, broadcast F_2=1 to p_1 and p_3. When receives T_2 from RP_2; RP_1 calculates diff= $U_{12}-T_{21}$=1-0=1, sends M<p_1, 1, m_0> to RP_2; RP_3 calculate diff= $U_{32}-T_{23}$=1-0=1, sends M<P_3, 5, m_2> to RP_2. Then, RP_2

rearranges messages: $<p_1, LC_1=1, m_0>$, $<p_3, LC_3=5, m_2>$. Then, RP_2 rolls back p_2 to its checkpoint B and sends the vector LC=[0,0,0] to p_2.

During message replaying of p_2, after receiving $<p_1, LC_1=1, m_0>$ from RP_2, p_2 sets LC:[1,2,0]. Then p_2 sends $<p_2$, $LC_2=3, m_1>$ to p_3. As AM. $LC_2=3$, $LC_2=3$, AM. $LC_2=LC_2$, thus p_3 discards m_1. After receiving $<p_3, 5, m_2>$ from RP_2, p_2 sets LC:[1,6,5]. Then, p_2 sends $<p_2, 7, m_3>$ to p_1, sets LC:[1,7,5]. After receiving $<p_2, LC_2=7, m_3>$ from p_2, as AM.LC_2 $=7$, $LC_2=7$, AM.$LC_2=LC_2$, thus p_1 discards this message. Then, RP_2 sends a message with $F_2=0$ to p_1 and p_3 to inform them p_2 is recovered from failure.

4.1.5 Correctness of the Protocol

Under PWD assumption, in a log-based rollback-recovery protocol, the execution of a process consists of a sequence of deterministic state intervals. A state interval is recoverable if the execution to be replayed can reach this interval, despite any future failures in the system [2].

Theorem 4-1. *If one or more processes are detected failure, they must be recovered under the recovery protocol.*

Proof. Because each message and their equivalent replayed order are previously saved in message log or stable storage, according to the recoverable notion of state interval, any failed processes can be recovered.

Case one. Suppose one process failed in the system. After the failure detected, the recovery process acquires all the messages received by the failed process in its normal execution by the message number check method. After these messages are rearranged by the logic clock of sender process, the receipt events of these messages can be executed again. So, the failed process must have been finally recovered from failure. As each process is recovered independently, if another failure occurs during its failure recovery or its future failure free execution, this failed process also can be recovered accordingly.

Case two. Suppose more than one processes have failed in the system. Because the failed processes can be recovered by recovery process individually, if more than one process failed, then they can be recovered respectively.

□

Theorem 4-2. *Under the recovery protocol, the global state is consistent after all the failed processes are recovered.*

Proof. If failures are detected in the system; not failed processes, or pause at the event of sending a message to failed processes, or continue to execute if it does not send messages to failed processes.

Case one. Suppose normal processes have not sent any message to failed processes. After the failed processes recover from failures, the number of messages that normal processes sent to the failed process does not change. The number of messages that failed process received from normal processes also does not change. According to the message number check theorem, the global state is consistent then.

Case two. Suppose normal processes pause at the events of sending message to failed processes. As normal processes have not sent any message to failed processes, so the global state then is also consistent after the failed processes are recovered. But after a process recovers from failure, there may be more than one message receiving events for it to execute. In fact, as these messages are sent by different processes; these messages have a different channel delay, have no logic dependent relation. So, the receiving events of these messages can be executed in any order without affecting the future execution of the system. □

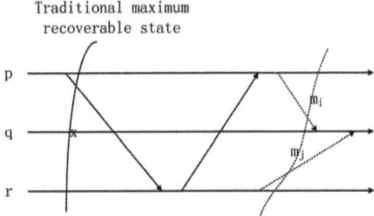

Figure 4.3 p and r go on running

For example, as shown in Figure 4.3, suppose q fails at "x". When q has been recovered from failure and reaches the dotted curve, it may execute $R(m_i)$ or execute $R(m_j)$. In fact, as $R(m_i) \xrightarrow{NAHB} R(m_j)$, these two events can be executed in any order. During recovery, log-based rollback-recovery protocols force the recovery execution of the process up to the maximum recoverable state. In this example, the traditional maximum recoverable state is the curve as shown in the Figure. In previous message logging protocols, normal processes have to pause at maximum recoverable state to wait failed processes to be recovered, because in the future the exact receipt order of the message is always wanted. In our protocol, as the *always-happens-before* relation is always held among receipt events, so normal process can go on running upon failures occurring.

4.1.6 Performance of the Protocol

In our protocol, as the equivalent receipt order of each message is logged by the sender process, so the *no-orphan-condition* is always held during processes normal execution. That is, our protocol implements such property that $\forall m$, $\neg stable(R(m)) \Rightarrow |Depend(R(m))|=0$. So, our protocol has the same advantage just as pessimistic and Causal protocols in failure recovery. The output commit is fast; because there is no any orphan process in the system, the output messages can be sent to the outside of the world without coordinating with other process. The recovery of failed processes is simply because only the failed processes are rolled back. As the messages to be replayed are confined to such received messages since a checkpoint is set up, each process needs only take one checkpoint.

Our protocol has also gotten the advantage just like optimistic protocols in process normal execution [35, 36]. Unlike sender based message protocols [23, 24, 25], in our protocol after receiving a message, the receiver needs not send the message receipt order to the sender process. In process normal execution, the received message can be processed immediately, because the receiver process needs not visit stable storage.

Unlike Pessimistic and Causal protocols, during recovery of the failed processes, the normal processes can continue to run without waiting for the failed processes to be recovered. This property may be very useful in some area, such as wireless sensor networks.

The main disadvantage of our protocol may be that the message payload needs to be saved in stable storage before this message is sent out, which may slow down the delivery of the message.

35

Table 4.1   Comparison among message logging protocols

Comparison	Various message logging protocols			
	Pessimistic	Optimistic	Causal	Ours
Checkpoints	1	Several	1	1
Orphan processes	No	Possible	No	No
Roll back extent	Last checkpoint	Possibly several checkpoints	Last checkpoint	Last checkpoint
Information message piggyback	No	small	Middle or large	small
Recovery	Simplified	Complicate	Simplified	Simplified
Performance in Normal execution	bad	good	middle	good

The comparison of our recovery protocols to such protocols mentioned above is shown in table 4.1. Nearly in all properties as shown in table 4.1, our protocol is better than other protocols except the information piggybacked on each message. When sending a message to another process, our protocol must piggyback the logic clock on this message. While in Pessimistic protocols, the message to be sent needs not piggyback any information, but it must be to pay for the performance degradation because of synchronous message logging.

Compared with our previous protocol [35,36], the receiver process under this protocol needs not log any message when receiving messages because of the improvement of the algorithm. This further simplified the recovery algorithm.

Unlike other message logging recovery protocols, the normal processes in our protocol not only need not roll back, but also can go on running during failure recovery. This property is somewhat like forward recovery, when some processes failed the normal processes are ongoing execution without rolling back or stopping.

4.2 Find Recovery Line by Message Number Check

4.2.1 Introduction

Uncoordinated checkpointing allows each process to independently take its checkpoint in process normal execution. If failures occur, the failed process initiates the rollback by broadcasting a request message to collect the dependency information maintained by each process. Then it calculates the recovery line [14] and request all processes roll back to this line from which begins their execution. The traditional approaches to calculate recovery line are *rollback-dependency-graph* and *checkpoint-graph*, which are all drawn from the dependency information. Thus, the dependency information needs to be piggybacked on each message to be sent, which may degrade the performance of communication systems. On the other hand, it may increase the capacity demand for table storage if each process needs to take several checkpoints.

An alternated method to calculate recovery line is to check the number of messages received and sent in a global checkpoint to determine if it is the recovery line demanded. By theorem 2-3, if $\forall i,\ T_{ii}^{(ti)} \geq \sum\limits_{j \neq i, j=1,2...n} T_{ji}^{(tj)}$, $G\ (t_1, t_2...t_n)$ is

a consistent global checkpoint. Thus, if each p_i saves T_i with its checkpoint, consistence of global checkpoint, which consists of each process checkpoint, can be determined by checking the message number recorded in the T matrix then.

4.2.2 System Modal and Main Data Structure

A distributed system is a set of processes, which consists of P_1, P_2,... P_n. P_i, i=1, 2,... n, do not share a common memory. The communication subsystem receives messages reliably and in FIFO order. Each of the messages is received after an arbitrary finite delay.

Each process P_i maintains a n-vector $T_i = [T_{i1}, T_{i2}, ... T_{in}]$ in its volatile memory.

4.2.3 Description of the Algorithm

In its normal execution, for each process P_i, after sending a message to P_j, $T_{ii} \leftarrow T_{ii}+1$; after receiving a message m from P_j, $T_{ij} \leftarrow T_{ij}$ +1. When taking a checkpoint, P_i save $T_i = [T_{i1}, T_{i2},...T_{in}]$ with this checkpoint. Then P_i sends broadcast messages to every P_j to request T_j. After receiving the request message from P_i, as P_j may have taken several checkpoints, it sends all the T_j which saved with each checkpoint $C_{j,u}$, u=1,2..., to P_i. After receiving all responding messages from each P_j, P_i calculates the most recent consistent global checkpoint from the message number information obtained from each process by theorem 2-3. If the recovery line exists, P_i Save the information of this recovery line on stable storage. And then, P_i sends the checkpoint index x of $C_{j,x}$ which belongs to P_j and is contained in the recovery line to P_j. Then, all the processes in the system delete the checkpoints which are previously taken before the recovery line, as they are no use in the future.

The main algorithm is shown bellow.

For process P_i who takes a checkpoint:

When takes a checkpoint:

   k←k+1

   Take checkpoint $C_{i,k}$

   Save T_i with $C_{i,k}$,

   Broadcast message to P_j to request T_j

After receiving all response messages from P_j:

   Calculate the recovery line by all T_j, j=1,2...n

   If the recovery line exists

      Save the information of this recovery line

      Sends x to P_j

      ; x is the checkpoint index of $C_{j,x}$ contained

      ; in recovery line

      Delete all checkpoints previously taken before $C_{i,m}$

      ; $C_{i,m}$ is the checkpoint of p_i in the recovery line

For process P_j:

After receiving a broadcast from P_i:

Sends all T_j, which saved with $C_{j,u}$, $u=1,2...$, to P_i

; There may be several T_j if P_j takes several checkpoints

When received a checkpoint index x:

Delete all checkpoints previously taken before $C_{j,x}$

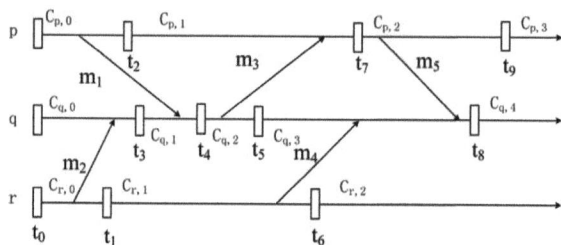

Figure 4.4 An example of the algorithm

As an example of the algorithm, see Figure 4.4. Process r broadcasts request message to p and q, after it takes checkpoint $C_{r,1}$, suppose $C_{q,1}^{(t3)}$ and $C_{p,1}^{(t2)}$ have not been taken then. After receives $T_p^{(t0)}=[0,0,0]$ and $T_q^{(t0)}=[0,0,0]$, As $T_{pp}^{(t0)}=0$, $T_{qp}^{(t0)}=0$, $T_{rp}^{(t1)}=0$, $T_{pp}^{(t0)}=$ $T_{pp}^{(t0)}+T_{rp}^{(t1)}$; $T_{qq}^{(t0)}=0$, $T_{pq}^{(t0)}=0$, $T_{rq}^{(t1)}=0$, $T_{qq}^{(t0)}=$ $T_{pq}^{(t0)}+T_{rq}^{(t1)}$; $T_{rr}^{(t1)}=1$, $T_{pr}^{(t0)}=0$, $T_{qr}^{(t0)}=0$, $T_{rr}^{(t1)}>$ $T_{qr}^{(t0)}+T_{rr}^{(t1)}$, $G(t_0,t_0,t_1)$ is a consistent global checkpoint. So, r deletes its checkpoint $C_{r,0}$ afterwards, and saves $T_r^{(t1)}$ with $C_{r,1}$. Accordingly, after $C_{p,1}$ is taken, $G(t_2,t_0,t_1)$ is consistent, p deletes $C_{p,0}$; after $C_{q,1}$ is taken, $G(t_2,t_3,t_1)$ is consistent, q deletes $C_{q,0}$; after $C_{q,2}$ is taken, $G(t_2,t_4,t_1)$ is consistent, q deletes $C_{q,1}$; after $C_{q,3}$ is taken, $G(t_2,t_5,t_1)$ is consistent, q deletes $C_{q,2}$. After $C_{r,2}$ is taken, $G(t_2,t_5,t_6)$ is consistent, r deletes $C_{r,1}$. After $C_{p,2}$ is taken, $G(t_7,t_5,t_6)$ is consistent, p deletes $C_{p,1}$. After $C_{q,4}$ is taken, as $G(t_7,t_8,t_6)$ is not consistent, q maintains $C_{q,3}$ and $C_{q,4}$ on stable storage simultaneously. After $C_{p,3}$ is taken, q sends $T_q^{(t5)}$ and $T_q^{(t8)}$ to p; r sends $T_r^{(t6)}$ to p. Then, p calculates recovery line from $T_q^{(t5)}$, $T_q^{(t8)}$, $T_r^{(t6)}$, $T_p^{(t7)}$ and $T_p^{(t9)}$; as $G(t_7,t_5,t_6)$ and $G(t_9,t_8,t_6)$ are all consistent global checkpoints, but $G(t_9,t_8,t_6)$ is the most recent one. So, the checkpoints $C_{p,2}$ and $C_{q,3}$ will be deleted afterwards. In this way, the most recent consistent global checkpoint if it exists can be calculated by this algorithm at the time after a checkpoint is taken.

4.2.4 Correctness of the Algorithm

Theorem 4-3. *After one or more checkpoints are taken at any time, the recovery line can be found by the algorithm if the recovery line exists then.*

Proof.

Case one, suppose that processes alternately take a checkpoint during process normal execution. In this case, only one process takes a checkpoint at any time. Because all the information of T_j has been collected by a process after it takes checkpoint, if the recovery line exists, then it must be found by using theorem 2-2.

Case two, suppose that more processes take checkpoints simultaneously during process normal execution. In this case, because the recovery line is the most recently consistent global checkpoint, any processes who take checkpoint cannot delete its local checkpoint which contained by the recovery line after it takes checkpoint. So, if the recovery line exists, it must be found by one of the processes who take a checkpoint. □

4.2.5 Comparison with other Algorithms

Compared with other approaches, the *rollback-dependency-graph* [15] and *checkpoint-graph* [16] need to piggyback extra information with each message sent. And in these approaches, each process needs to maintain many checkpoints in stable storage, after a long running of the system the capacity demand for stable storage will be greatly increased. The algorithm with message number check needs not piggyback any extra information on each message, and each process always maintains such checkpoints that may be useful in the future. Upon failures occur, the processes can fast roll back to the recovery line without any coordinating action to find where to roll back. The main disadvantage of the algorithm may be the cost to pay for finding the recovery line when a process takes checkpoint. If a process frequently takes checkpoint, this may degrade the performance of process normal execution.

In this chapter, we introduce a message logging protocol and an algorithm to explain how to use the theorems and methods on chapter 2 and chapter 3. The protocol and algorithm can be further improved under different applying environment. Such as, in the message logging protocol, if the system is on a fast network, the sender process can log the message determinants in a unique message log not in local one. Thus, the recovery process RP_i can visit this unique log directly without coordinating with other recovery process RP_j. We hope these algorithms are useful to the study of rollback recovery and find more use in the corresponding applications.

References

[1]ALVISI, L. AND MARZULLO, K. 1998. "Message logging:pessimistic, optimistic, causal and optimal," IEEE Trans. Softw. Eng. 24, 2, 149–159.

[2] Elnozahy E N, Alvisi L, Wang Yimin, et al. "A Survey of Rollback recovery Protocols in Message passing Systems," ACM Computing Surveys, 2002, 34(3): 375-408.

[3] SCHLICHTING, R. D. AND SCHNEIDER, F. B. 1983. "Fail-stop processors: An approach to designing fault-tolerant computing systems," ACM Trans. Comput. Syst. 1, 3, 222–238.

[4] CHANDY, M. AND LAMPORT, L. 1985. "Distributed snapshots: Determining global states of distributed systems," ACM Trans. Comput. Syst. 31, 1, 63–75.

[5] STROM, R. AND YEMINI, S. 1985. "Optimistic recovery in distributed systems," ACMTrans. Comput. Syst. 3, 3, 204–226.

[6] Helary J-M.Netzer, R.Raynal, H.B. "Consistency issues in distributed checkpoints," IEEE Transactions on Software Engineering, vol. 25, no. 2, pp. 274-281, March 1999.

[7] JOHNSON, D. B. 1989. "Distributed System Fault Tolerance Using Message Logging and Checkpointing," Ph.D. Thesis, Rice University, Department of Computer Science.

[8] Y. Deng, E.K. Park. "Checkpointing and rollback-recovery algorithms in distributed systems," J. Systems Software 4 (1994) 59–71

[9] R. Koo and S. Toueg. "Checkpointing and Roll-back Recovery for Distributed Systems," IEEE Transactions on Software Engineering, pp. 23–31, January 1987.

[10] E.N. Elnozahy, W. Zwaenepoel, "Manetho: Transparent Roll Back-Recovery with Low Overhead, Limited Rollback, and Fast Output Commit," IEEE Transactions on Computers, vol. 41, no. 5, pp. 526-531, May 1992.

[11] L.M. Silva, J.G. Silva. "Global checkpointing for distributed programs," Proc. 11th Symp. on Reliable Distributed Systems, Houston, 1992, pp. 155–162.

[12] B. Randell. "System Structure for Fault Tolerance," IEEE Transactions on Software Engineering. SE- 1 : 220-232, 1975.

[13] D. L. Russell. "State Restoration in Systems of Communicating Processes," IEEE Transactions on Software Engineering. 6 (2): 183-194. March 1980.

[14] Y. M. Wang, A. Lowry, and W. K. Fuchs, "Consistentglobal checkpoints based on direct dependencytracking," Research ReportRC 18465, IBM T.J. Watson Research Center. Yorktown Heights, New York, Oct. 1992.

[15] BHARGAVA, B. AND LIAN, S. R. 1988. "Independent checkpointing and concurrent rollback for recovery—An optimistic approach," In Proceedings, Seventh Symposium on Reliable Distributed Systems, 3–12.

[16] Y.M. Wang, A. Lowry, and W.K. Fuchs, "Consistent Global Checkpoints Based on Direct Dependency Tracking," Information Processing Letters, vol. 50, no. 4, pp. 223-230, May 1993.

[17] J. M. Helary, A. Mostefaoui and M. Raynal. "Virtual precedence in asynchronous systems: concepts and applications," In Proceedings of the 11th Workshop on Distributed Algorithms. LNCS press, 1997.

[18] R. Netzer and J.Xu. "Necessary and Suffcient Conditions for Consistent Global Snapshots," Technical Report

93-32, Department of Computer Sciences, Brown University, July 1993.

[19] L. Alvisi and K. Marzullo, "Message Logging: Pessimistic, Optimistic, Causal, and Optimal," IEEE Trans. Software Eng., vol. 24, no. 2, pp. 149-159, Feb. 1998.

[20] Taesoon P. Namyoon W. Heon Y. Yeom. "An Efficient Optimistic Message Logging Scheme for the Recoverable Mobile Computing Systems," IEEE TRANSACTIONS ON MOBILE COMPUTING, VOL. 1, NO. 4, pp 265-277, OCTOBER-DECEMBER 2002.

[21] JOHNSON, D. B. AND ZWAENEPOEL, W. "Senderbased message logging," In Digest of Papers, FTCS-17, The Seventeenth Annual International Symposium on Fault-Tolerant Computing, 14–19, 1987..

[22] M. L. Powell and D. L. Presotto. Publishing: "A reliable broadcast communication mechanism," In Proc. of the 9th International Symposium on Operating System Principles, pp. 100-109, 1983.

[23] A. Bouteiller, F. Cappello, T. Hérault, G. Krawezik, P.Lemarinier and F. Magniette. MPICH-V2: "a Fault Tolerant MPI for Volatile Nodes based on Pessimistic Sender Based Message Logging," In Proc. of the 15th International Conference on High Performance Networking and Computing(SC2003), November 2003.

[24] D. B. Johnson and W. Zwaenpoel. "Sender-Based Message Logging," In Digest of Papers: 17th International Symposium on Fault-Tolerant Computing, pp. 14-19, 1987.

[25] J. Xu, R.B. Netzer and M. Mackey. "Sender-based message logging for reducing rollback propagation," In Proc. of the 7th International Symposium on Parallel and Distributed Processing, pp. 602-609, 1995.

[26] JOHNSON, D. B. AND ZWAENEPOEL,W. 1988. "Recovery in distributed systems using optimistic message logging and checkpointing," In Proceedings of the Sixth Annual ACM Symposium on Principles of Distributed Computing (PODC-88), 171–181.

[27] SISTLA, A. AND WELCH, J. 1989. "Efficient distributed recovery using message logging," In Proceedings of the 8th Annual ACM Symposium on Principles of Distributed Computing (PODC), 223–238.

[28] ALVISI, L. 1996. "Understanding the Message Logging Paradigm for Masking Process Crashes," Ph.D. Thesis, Cornell University, Department of Computer Science.

[29] ELNOZAHY, E. N. 1993. "Manetho: Fault Tolerance in Distributed Systems using Rollback-Recovery and Process Replication," Ph.D. Thesis, Rice University, Department of Computer Science.

[30] Gao, X. Li and R.H Zhang, "The Extended Finite State Machine and Fault Tolerant Mechanism in Distributed System," Proc 7th ACIS International Conference on Software Engineering Research, Management and Applications, Dec. 2009, pp. 33-38, doi:10.1109/SERA.2009.33.

[31] M. Aminian, M.k. A kbari and B. Javadi, "Coordinated Checkpoint from Message Payload in Pessimistic Sender-Based Message Logging," Proc 20th international conference on Parallel and distributed processing, Apr 2006, doi:10.1109/IPDPS.2006.1639619.

[32] A. Bouteiller, T. Ropars, G. Bosilca, C. Morin and J. Dongarra, "Reasons for a Pessimistic or Optimistic Message Logging Protocol in MPI Uncoordinated Failure Recovery," Proc. Cluster Computing and Workshops, IEEE International Conference,Sept. 2009, pp. 1–9, doi: 10.1109/CLUSTR. 2009.5289157.

[33] E. Meneses, G. Bronevetsky and L.V. Kale, "Evaluation of Simple Causal Message Logging for Large-Scale Fault

Tolerant HPC," Proc. Systems Parallel and Distributed Processing Workshops and Phd Forum 1540, doi: 10.1109/IPDPS.2011.307.

[34] E. Meneses, L.V. Kale and G. Bronevetsky, "Dynamic Load Balance for Optimized Message Logging in Fault Tolerant HPC Applications," Proc IEEE International on Cluster Computing 2011, Sept. 2011, pp: 281-289, doi:10.1109/CLUSTER.2011.39.

[35] Shengfa Gao, Jing Cai, Zhen Feng. "Optimistic message logging based on message rearranging and message number check," PRC, 201210239710.0 [p], 2012. 7. 3

[36] Jing Cai, Shengfa Gao. "Message Rearrange Theory in Message Recovery Protocol," 2013 5th International Conference on Computer Science and Information Technology (CSIT) , pp. 293-297

Printed by Books on Demand GmbH, Norderstedt / Germany